Here We Are

Here We Are

MY FRIENDSHIP WITH PHILIP ROTH

BENJAMIN TAYLOR

PENGUIN BOOKS

I wish to thank The Corporation of Yaddo for their generous hospitality. Three works of criticism were before me as I wrote this book: Roth Unbound *by Claudia Roth Pierpont,* Philip Roth's Rude Truth *by Ross Posnock and* Philip Roth *by Hermione Lee. Chapter one, "No Model but Itself," appeared in somewhat different form in* Harper's Magazine.

—*B. T.*

PENGUIN BOOKS
An imprint of Penguin Random House LLC
penguinrandomhouse.com

Library of Congress Cataloging-in-Publication Data

Names: Taylor, Benjamin, 1952– author.
Title: Here we are : my friendship with Philip Roth / Benjamin Taylor.
Description: New York : Penguin Books, 2020.
Identifiers: LCCN 2020002291 (print) | LCCN 2020002292 (ebook) |
ISBN 9780525505242 (hardcover) | ISBN 9780525505259 (ebook)
Subjects: LCSH: Roth, Philip—Friends and associates. |
Novelists, American—20th century—Biography. | Taylor, Benjamin,
1952—Friends and associates. | Authors, American—20th century—Biography.
Classification: LCC PS3568.O855 Z935 2020 (print) |
LCC PS3568.O855 (ebook) | DDC 813/.54—dc23
LC record available at https://lccn.loc.gov/2020002291
LC ebook record available at https://lccn.loc.gov/2020002292

Printed in the United States of America
3 5 7 9 10 8 6 4 2

Set in Janson MT Pro

To Dr. Richard Friedman—

without whom not

The stupendous decimation that is death sweeping us all away. Orchestra, audience, conductor, technicians, swallows, wrens—think of the numbers for Tanglewood alone just between now and the year 4000. Then multiply that times everything. The ceaseless perishing. What an idea! What maniac conceived it? And yet what a lovely day it is today, a gift of a day, a perfect day lacking nothing.

—THE HUMAN STAIN

CONTENTS

CHAPTER ONE

No Model but Itself ■ 1

CHAPTER TWO

The Dignity of an Elderly Gentleman ■ 15

CHAPTER THREE

Mistakes ■ 37

CHAPTER FOUR

Housekeeping in America ■ 61

CHAPTER FIVE

There Is a God and His Name Is Laughter ■ 81

CHAPTER SIX

The Destructive Element ■ 107

CHAPTER SEVEN

Why Must the Atheists' Booth Look So Sad? ■ 133

CHAPTER EIGHT

Partings ■ 151

Here We Are

Philip Roth

March 19, 1933 – May 22, 2018

The Austin, 130 West 79th Street, Manhattan

Philip Roth was among the greatest American writers of any generation. He published thirty-one books of fiction, memoir, and essays. More than half were worked on here-his studio, then his residence-from 1988 until his death. He received numerous national and international awards, some several times, from the beginning to the end of his career: among them, the Pulitzer Prize, the National Book Award, the PEN/Faulkner Award, the Man Booker International Prize, and the National Humanities Medal. He was celebrated around the world. He, in turn, championed the work of others: voices of dissent from Eastern Europe, overlooked artists of his generation, dozens of younger writers. Roth's enduring masterworks include *Goodbye, Columbus* (1959), *Portnoy's Complaint* (1969), *The Ghost Writer* (1979), *The Counterlife* (1986), *Sabbath's Theater* (1995), *American Pastoral* (1997), *The Human Stain* (2000), *The Plot Against America* (2004), and *Nemesis* (2010). The writer was as fierce as the man was generous: an enemy of cant, and an advocate of freedom in all its guises, personal and political.

Historic Landmarks Preservation Center

CHAPTER ONE

NO MODEL BUT ITSELF

Die in your prime and it is tragic. Die in your ninth decade and it is the debt paid, the quittance. Grief for those struck down too soon goes on and on. We are helplessly haunted by what might have been; a penumbra of vanished possibilities surrounds untimely death. But grief for the elderly is formal, stately. Most of all it is end-oriented.

You roll a boulder across the mouth of the cave.

You move on.

———————

In *The Ghost Writer*, Nathan Zuckerman says of Felix Abravanel that the master's charm was "a moat so oceanic that you could not even see the great turreted and buttressed thing it had been dug to protect." Philip too could seem a beguiling but remote citadel: august, many-towered, lavishly defended. Those who reached the inner keep met there someone quite different from the persona devised for public purposes. Still vitally present at home was the young man he'd remained all along, full of satirical hijinks and gleeful ventriloquisms and antic fun building to crescendos. Imaginary relatives were a specialty. I recall for example Paprika Roth, a retired stripper living in the Florida Panhandle. A glint in the eye told you hilarity was on the road.

"Ben, do you remember when Mrs. Fischbein was on *The $64,000 Question?*"

"A little before my time, Philip."

"Well, Mrs. Fischbein had walloped the competition. She'd advanced to the sixty-four-thousand-dollar question itself. Came the drum roll and the announcer said, 'For sixty-four thousand dollars, Mrs. Fischbein, who was—the first man?' 'I wouldn't tell you for a million dollars!' cried Mrs. Fischbein."

The place of origin, Newark's Weequahic section, was his Great Code and Rosetta stone. I mean Weequahic as endlessly rediscovered through alchemical imagination, that flame turned up under experience for the smelting of novels. "Ours was not a neighborhood steeped in darkness," says Zuckerman in *American Pastoral*. "The place was bright with industriousness. There was a big belief in life and we were steered relentlessly in the direction of success: a better existence was going to be ours . . . Am I wrong to think we delighted in living there? No delusions are more familiar than those inspired in the elderly by nostalgia, but am I completely mistaken to think that living as well-born children in Renaissance Florence could not have held a candle to growing up within aromatic range of Tabachnik's pickle barrels? Am I mistaken to think that even back then, in the vivid present, the fullness of life stirred our emotions to an extraordinary extent? Has anywhere since so engrossed you in its ocean of details? The *detail*, the immensity of the detail, the force of the detail, the weight of the detail—the rich endlessness of detail surrounding you in your young life like the six feet of dirt that'll be packed on your grave when you're dead."

Philip spent his final three weeks in the cardiac intensive-care unit at New York-Presbyterian Hospital. A lot of women and a smattering of men surrounded him. We were friends, lovers, protégés, relatives, employees, representing every decade of his adult life. (This I know: When my time comes, the waiting room will not be crowded with ex-lovers.)

On the twenty-first day, the attending came out of Philip's room and said: "He is *philosopher*, no?"

"Yes," I said. And so it really was. Amid the general weeping, Philip was Socratic, as if instructing us, his loved ones, in how to die. He even remembered, like Socrates, a small debt owed—to Mrs. Solano, his housekeeper.

Near the end he asked for a moment alone with me and said something I wrote down as soon as I decently could: "I have been to see the great enemy, and walked around him, and talked to him, and he is not to be feared. I promise."

There had been earlier brushes with the great enemy, any one of which might have proved fatal. One occurred on August 22, 2012. Canadian geese were starting south. We'd gone to Litchfield for dinner and dressed up a bit for the occasion. Philip was in a sports jacket he claimed to have bought with the earnings from *Goodbye, Columbus.* (It may nearly have been so; he cared nothing for clothes.) Seated in our usual booth at the West Street Grill, we ordered the special soup, their gazpacho, sweet and crunchy with the local beefsteaks and cucumbers. I had a baseball question on the tip of my tongue: What was the name of "the natural," the player shot by a lady stalker in a Chicago hotel room? He gave me an amused look that darkened into puzzlement, then fear.

Then he pitched forward into the soup, unconscious. Too astounded for anything but composure, I summoned the management. Medics appeared almost immediately. As if by further magic, a stretcher sprang up from the floor to receive him, who though all but comatose was saying something: an attempt, entirely characteristic, at telling the medics how to do their job.

Moments later I was in the front seat of the ambulance beside the driver, with Philip and the two medics behind us. "Thready pulse," said one to the other. And then, to the driver: "Better turn on the siren." I thought, here is how it ends, and considered whom I would contact first. Thomas Mann's Aschenbach and the last line of *Death in Venice* came to mind, proving literature matters even in an emergency: "Before nightfall," writes Mann, "a shocked and respectful world received the news of his decease." Philip had equipped several of us with detailed instructions on how every aspect of his burial and memorial service should be handled. My mind veered to these.

Twenty minutes after our arrival at Charlotte Hungerford Hospital in Torrington, the ER physician explained that what Philip had suffered was an accumulated reaction to one of the drugs he'd been taking. When I entered the examining room Philip said, "No more books." At first I didn't know what he meant. What he meant, I shortly realized, was that *Nemesis*, his thirty-first, published two years earlier, would be his last. Thus he announced his retirement.

"You look right good for back from the dead," I told him.

"Just so we're clear," he said, "I did die." He had the sweetest smile sometimes. Now he took up the story he hadn't got to at dinner: In the summer of 1949, Eddie Waitkus, lefty All-Star with the Cubs, the Phillies, the Orioles and the Phillies again, was shot by a deranged admirer, Ruth Ann Steinhagen, in her room at the Edgewater Beach Hotel, to which she'd coaxed him with a letter: "Please come soon. I won't take much of your time. I promise."

Good as her word, she plugged him when he came through the door. Ruth Ann's plan had evidently been to shoot herself too in a Mayerling-style bloodbath, but she told the cops afterward that she couldn't find another bullet.

Eddie survived but never got his game back. Ruth Ann reported that after she shot him he'd said: "What'd you do that for, baby?" He spent the rest of his days wondering and died at fifty-three of esophageal cancer. Ruth Ann served a year in the madhouse at Kankakee and, released to the care of family, lived uneventfully for decades on Chicago's North Side, waiving off all queries.

What proved evergreen was "What'd you do that

for, baby?"—endlessly applicable and between Philip and me a fresh source of laughter each time one of us said it. Is the quick of friendship here, in finding the same things lastingly funny? Because it was he, because it was I? "Such a friendship has no model but itself," says Montaigne, "and can only be compared to itself . . . And is some mysterious quintessence." Because it was he. Because it was I.

There was no dramatic arc to our life together. It was not like a marriage, still less like a love affair. It was as plotless as friendship ought to be. We spent thousands of hours in each other's company. He was fully half my life. I cannot hope for another such friend.

One of the many authors Philip read in his years of retirement was himself, everything from Brenda Patimkin asking Neil Klugman to hold her glasses to Bucky Cantor teaching his playground charges, thirty books later, how to throw the javelin. I believe he took a death-defying satisfaction in the vastness of what he'd wrought, a shelf of work

augmenting the soul of the nation and built to out-
last whatever unforeseeable chances and changes
await us and our descendants.

"And then he hurled the javelin," Philip wrote at
journey's end. "You could see each of his muscles
bulging when he released it into the air. He let out
a strangulated yowl of effort . . . a noise expressing
the essence of him—the naked battle cry of striving
excellence . . . Running with the javelin aloft, stretch-
ing his throwing arm back behind his body, bringing the throwing arm through to release the javelin
high over his shoulder—and releasing it then like
an explosion—he seemed to us invincible."

At home on West Seventy-Ninth Street

CHAPTER TWO

THE DIGNITY OF
AN ELDERLY GENTLEMAN

Delirious near the end, he said, "We're going to the Savoy!"—surely the jauntiest dying words on record. But it was Riverside Memorial Chapel, the Jewish funeral parlor at Amsterdam and Seventy-Sixth, we were bound for. I was obliged to reidentify the body once we arrived there from New York-Presbyterian. A lady undertaker pointed the way to the viewing room and said: "You may stay for as long as you like. But do not touch him." Duly draped, Philip looked serene on his plinth—like a Roman emperor, one of the good ones. I pulled up a chair and managed to say, "Here we are." Here we are at the promised end. A phrase from *The Human*

Stain came to me: "the dignity of an elderly gentleman free from desire who behaves correctly." I wanted to tell him he was doing fine, that he was a champ at being dead, bringing to it all the professionalism he'd brought to previous tasks.

To talk daily with someone of such gifts had been a salvation. I'm not who I'd have been without him. "We've laughed so hard," he said to me some years ago. "Maybe write a book about our friendship." I take this as my warrant and write here without reticence, knowing the truth to be all that matters now.

Our conversation was about everything—novels, politics, families, dreams, sex, baseball, food, ex-friends, ex-lovers. But our keynote was American history, for which Philip was ravenous, consuming one big scholarly book after another. He became a great writer in the course of the eighties and especially the nineties when his novels became history-haunted. In the American trilogy, *American Pastoral*, *I Married a Communist* and *The Human Stain*, the heroes, Swede Levov, Ira Ringold and Coleman Silk, are solid men taken to pieces when the blindsiding force of history comes to call. Such was Philip's mature theme: unpredictable brutalities at large in the world and the illusoriness of ever being safe from them.

In keeping with the unseemliness of my profession (as he would say) I'd been taking notes all along. A lot of conversation got squirreled away. "Memories of the past," he wrote, "are not memories of facts but memories of your imaginings of the facts." Still, what I am struggling for in these pages is the fact of Philip as he was. He doesn't need me or anyone to ornament him. Imagination in memoir may indeed be inevitable, but I am treating it here as a trespasser and have tried at every turn to bar the way.

Writing a novel makes a god of you. Writing a memoir does not. This book is a nonfiction portrait and strives to be nothing else. In this kind of portraiture, the facts, not how you can metamorphose them, are what count—metamorphosis of the facts, the cardinal virtue of fiction, being the cardinal sin of memoir. Philip writes: "What one chooses to reveal in fiction is governed by a motive fundamentally aesthetic; we judge the author of a novel by how well he or she tells the story. But we judge morally the author of an autobiography, whose governing motive is primarily ethical as against aesthetic. How close is the narration to the truth? Is the author hiding his or her motives, presenting his or her actions and thoughts to lay bare the essential nature of conditions or trying to hide something, telling in order *not* to tell?" Is the author's presumed candor in fact a dance of the seven veils? All I can say is I am trying here for candor alone.

One day I reported on a strange case I'd been reading about. A man named Thomas Beer, who was Stephen Crane's first biographer, wove a tissue of creative lies, inventing loves and friendships that never were, even concocting virtuoso letters from Crane. It was fiction posing as fact. A succession of

Crane scholars went charging down Beer's blind alleys.

"May his bad example haunt you," Philip said.

He was genuinely puzzled by gossips. "All the fun of a secret is in keeping it. Why blab?" Maybe he took this view because he'd been more victimized by gossip than other people. He was oversensitive and sometimes mistook genuine concern for idle chatter. One mutual friend particularly drew fire for talking to anyone who'd listen about a recent operation Philip had undergone. Orthopedic surgeries could be openly reported, but cardiac procedures were confidential. "Can you imagine? He told five more people after I told him to stop. All of whom called this afternoon." In our friend's defense, I said his gossiping was like a locomotive and could stop only gradually.

Secrets and deceptions of every kind appealed to

Philip. He was not averse to cuckolding inattentive husbands. More wholesome opportunities for subterfuge were catnip too. Some years ago when I was submitting for publication a novel I'd written, he suggested I employ a pseudonym. We settled on Shoshana Lipshitz, a winner by the sound of the curriculum vitae we concocted: four years at Hotchkiss, women's studies and astronomy at Harvard, an internship at *The Paris Review*, Romance languages, European wanderings, the whole bit. We decided she was very pretty, a Natalie Portman type. To top it off, I proposed an archeological year in Mesoamerica but Philip said we were getting carried away.

"Maybe publishers won't like being fooled like this," I said. "They know how to google." For our part, we googled what turned out to be a small army of Shoshana Lipshitzes, variously active in the world. Thus our ruse, doomed to quick exposure had we launched it, died at birth.

While he was my best friend, and I his, there

were rooms in the fortress of secrets marked P. Roth that I know I was excluded from. This goes both ways, but he was an incomparable student of inner lives, of what's invisibly afoot. He managed to figure out more about me than I ever could about him. It need hardly be said that we weren't equals, and not just because he was twenty years older. His love acted on me, as on everyone, like a truth serum. He possessed the terrible gift of intimacy. He caused people to tell things they told no one else. His mineral-hard stare was impossible to hide from.

"Something's not right with you. Don't bother saying you're okay because you're not. Just say what's going on."

I told him it was bleakness. The shine had gone out of everything. Strangulation in the viscera; no food seemed edible. Once or twice, to my shame, I'd gone to bed hoping a heart attack would finish me. In a word, I was ill.

Here was the sort of assignment Philip reveled in. He got me to his psychiatrist within twenty-four hours. "Tell him exactly what you told me. He'll fix you up. Don't tell him about how Momma burned the roast in '57 and Daddy got so mad. He's not that kind of doctor." I had thought anxiety and depression were mutually exclusive. Our doctor told me they go together like Rogers and Astaire. He fixed me up with sertraline and olanzapine and may have saved my life. But the drugs have made me tearless. An odd side effect. At the Riverside Chapel, seated beside the dead man I adored, I found I could not cry.

I can't be the first gay man to have been an older straight man's mainstay. Philip had searched diligently for a beautiful young woman to see to him as Jane Eyre looked after old Mr. Rochester. What he got instead was me. The degree of attachment surprised us both. Were we lovers? Obviously not. Were we in love? Not exactly. Sufficient to say that ours was a conversation neither could have done without. Twelve years ago I saw him through his last love, for a young person less than half his age whose family strongly disapproved of the association and who evidently grew to disapprove of it herself. It was a trauma that might have plowed Philip under and that he tells aslant in *Exit Ghost*, the novel dedicated to me. After that came a couple of misguided attempts at courtship, painful for the women involved. Then he closed the door on erotic life altogether. He'd learned how to be an elderly gentleman who behaves correctly. He'd joined the ranks of the sexually abdicated.

I say: "I think I've worshipped at the altar of Eros long enough. I think my dues are paid."

"Wait till you go well and truly to sleep where the body forks. A great peacefulness, yes. But it's the harbinger of night. You're left to browse back through the enticements and satisfactions and agonies that were your former vitality—when you were strong in the sexual magic."

Why was the public so exceptionally interested in his personal life? E. L. Doctorow inspired no such curiosity. Neither has Alice Munro nor Toni

Morrison nor Cormac McCarthy. Gossip about Cynthia Ozick is hard to come by. About Don De-Lillo it is nil. Philip was something else altogether. True, Salinger comes to mind, chiefly because of the refusal to come out of hiding. Like Salinger, like Frost, like Hemingway, Philip generated a carapace that became a myth. In Frost's case, it was the farmer poet. In Hemingway's, the sportsman artist. In Salinger's, the wrathful recluse determined to give his readers nothing more.

In Philip's case, the Jewish good boy traduced by inner anarchy. Despite all the shifts and guises of fiction, it has been not so much protagonists as the man himself who, in book after book, keeps barging into the public eye, provoking adulation, hatred, learned commentary, everything but indifference. As with few other writers, readers have felt admitted to an inner sanctum they feel strongly about. At dinner one night in an Indian restaurant on Broadway, the actor Richard Thomas, spruce in a white beard, said to Philip: "You're the writer who's meant most to me." (As I've had a case on Richard Thomas since he was John-Boy on *The Waltons*, the whole scene was heady.) Some variant of the encounter occurred when we went to any public place. Particularly on the Upper West Side. "Let's have dinner on the East Side," Philip would occasionally say. "Nobody knows me over there." Prompt refutation came in a favorite eatery on Third when a woman at the bar beckoned to me with a long forefinger. "Young man, is that Philip Roth you're with?" I nodded. She passed me her card. "Tell him I've got a classic six on Park and am available."

Prior to the 1980s, he'd just been one of the interesting writers. Some of his books meant little to me—*The Breast*, for instance, which is lousy any way you look at it. But then came marvels like *The Ghost Writer*, *The Counterlife*, *Operation Shylock* and *Sabbath's Theater*, proving him the best American novelist of his generation, our likeliest candidate for immortality. It was 1994, the year he finished *Sabbath*, that I met Philip. The occasion was our friend

Joel Conarroe's sixtieth birthday. The venue was the James Beard House on West Twelfth Street. There was Philip, aglow and triumphant: the dogged athlete who'd rebounded from orthopedic and mental breakdown, the natural bachelor who'd extracted himself from untenable marriage, the tenacious self-reinventor who'd written *Sabbath*, his most scandalous book.

That night he was all speed and laughter—head thrown back—and supernaturally quick with the next line. He asked what I'd been reading. I said Bellow's *Herzog*. "Yes. That loaf of bread a rat has burrowed into, leaving his rat shape. Herzog cutting slices from the other end." Then he quoted a line from memory: "'But what do you want, Herzog?' 'But that's just it—not a solitary thing. I am pretty well satisfied to be, to be just as it is willed, and for as long as I may remain in occupancy.'" Before leaving he said, "Let's have lunch, kid"—but there was to be no lunch for years.

In the summer of 1998, after reading bound

proofs of *I Married a Communist,* I decided to write to him. I was struck particularly by the final pages where the narrator, Nathan Zuckerman, recalls his mother telling him that Grandpa has died and is now a star. "I searched the sky and said, 'Is he that one?' and she said yes, and we went back inside and I fell asleep." It makes sense anew to Nathan as an explanation of the dead, each of them a furnace burning away up there, "no longer impaled on their moment but dead and free of the traps set for them by their era." No more calumny or betrayal. No more idealism or hope. Just the blazing heavens, "that universe into which error does not obtrude."

A few days after I mailed my letter the phone rang. It was Philip wanting to talk. I felt at once that I was laughing with someone I knew well. Acrobatically unpredictable though the conversation was, I could follow his moves. Someone had to lead. Then he hung up without notice and I felt I'd been danced off the edge of the world.

Our first meal together, the first of hundreds,

was three years after that. I'd moved back to New York full-time and he was there seasonally. We decided to have the long-delayed lunch. He'd sent me *The Dying Animal* and proposed that we talk about it. I met him at a Thai restaurant called Rain at Columbus and Eighty-Second. The neighborhood around the Museum of Natural History had already been Philip's for more than twenty years.

"What do you think of my little book?"

Determined not to gush, I said that the scene where Consuela Castillo shows David Kepesh her doomed cancerous breasts reminded me of a similar scene in Solzhenitsyn's *Cancer Ward* in which a girl, on the night before her mastectomy, goes to the room of a boy sick with a cancer of his own and chastely asks him to worship her doomed right breast. "Today it was a marvel. Tomorrow it would be in the trash bin," I said, quoting Solzhenitsyn. In the silence that followed, I felt our friendship begin.

Early on he told me this: "What I care about is individuals enmeshed in some nexus of particulars.

Philosophical generalization is completely alien to me—some other writer's work. I'm a philosophical illiterate. All my brain power has to do with *specificity*, life's proliferating minutiae. Wouldn't know what to do with a general idea if it were hand-delivered. Would try to catch the FedEx man before he left the driveway. 'Wrong address, pal! Big ideas? No, thanks!'"

I mentioned a few characters of his whose intense particularity touches the universal: Mickey Sabbath, Swede Levov, Coleman Silk.

"Glad for the vote of confidence but I aim only at specifics. Entirely for others to say whether some universal has been hit. I have for instance never—I repeat, never—written a word about women in general. This will come as news to my harshest critics but it's true. Women, each one particular, appear in my books. But womankind is nowhere to be found."

I've got an earworm, Ben." Earworm: some (usually idiotic) tune that won't leave your head.

"There's only one thing to drive out a worm and that's another worm," I say and sing, "Lydia, oh, Lydia, oh have you met Lydia, Lydia the *tat*-tooed lady!"

"I think that worked," he says, shaking a finger in one ear. We're on our way to Alice Tully Hall to hear the Emerson Quartet. They're doing Shostakovich's string quartets in a series of evenings. Tonight is the conclusion.

Philip loves the intimacy of chamber music. Orchestral and classical vocal are not for him. The one time I got him to enjoy an opera it was Shostakovich's *The Nose*, hardly standard fare. Schoenberg's *Moses und Aron* he refers to as *Der Schmerz im Tuchas*. He does allow as Strauss's *Four Last Songs* are pretty good in the Schwarzkopf version. While he does not read music, he tends to grasp it in highly structural terms—exposition, development, reprise, et cetera—and has a remarkable musical memory, along with a quicksilver way of finding metaphors for what he's heard: "The scherzo is four madmen making up a dance as they go." "The cello is bearing a grudge." "The second violin is more confidential than the first."

Following intermission he is rigidly at attention for Shostakovich's Thirteenth. The elaborate *pizzicati* and strange slapping of the viola belly with the bow stick fascinate us both, as if composer and performers were trying to get at something more elemental than music.

Afterward, out on Broadway, we listen to a bespectacled, wild-haired, Upper West Side–type boy of about fourteen expostulating with his father: "No, Dad, the violist has to climb into *thirteenth* position to play the unison note with the violins!" The unison note, if that's what it's called, was indeed a keening voice to send us home with. "How about *that* for a worm?" Philip asks. "Don't think I'll ever get it out of my brainpan." Again he shakes a finger in his ear.

"Brainpan": I go home and write that down. All of life up there in the brainpan, all of it somehow husbanded there. In old age, waiting for sleep, Philip would pick a year and revisit it month by month, week by week, room by room. "It's all *there*. What happened is now the sum of me. A little patience and the locks turn. I'm back wherever I choose to go."

My own locks turn and I am at Philip's seventy-fourth birthday celebration. He'd said it would be tempting fate to hold out for seventy-five, so a seventy-fourth was planned at Judith Thurman's town house. The garden was tented in and a marvelous supper laid on. Afterward Philip asked, rather surprisingly, if anyone cared to recite a poem from memory. Mark Strand reeled off one of his own ("In a field, I am the absence of field"), then looked at me as if to say, "Your serve." What came to mind and I recited, stumbling only once or twice, was Frost's "I Could Give All to Time" with its stirring conclusion:

I could give all to Time except—except
What I myself have held. But why declare
The things forbidden that while the Customs slept
I have crossed to Safety with? For I am There,
And what I would not part with I have kept.

"Those rhymes!" said Philip on the phone the following morning. "It's as if nature made them."

A bread-and-butter note from Philip Guston

CHAPTER THREE

MISTAKES

I ask if I may take a few notes. "You were saying about the Newark of the thirties."

"It consisted of ethnic villages: Irish, Italian, Slav, Jewish. There was also a black neighborhood. And then, suddenly, it was December 7, 1941, and there was a current of feeling in all these villages that was stronger than what divided us. I think my sustained recollection dates from that afternoon. From then on, life became narrative rather than episodic. The onset of war was my starting point. I began to read the paper. The sound of Roosevelt's or Hitler's voice on the radio meant to me what it meant to the grown-ups, comfort or menace. And I remember understanding the fearsomeness of the banner headline CORREGIDOR FALLS, a shock to all my certainties. Home was safety. Home was bounty. I had no idea how little money we had, how few frills. I didn't know what an artichoke was till I left home. When Mrs. William F. Buckley Jr. said to me, 'What's your background?' I told her I didn't have one, we were too poor. We enjoyed a lower-middle-class way of life and had won the elusive prize of family concord. The emotional spectrum ran from contentment to extreme happiness. That such a range is not your typical raw stuff for the making of a writer goes without saying. But it was my raw stuff. I'd been blessed with the luckiest of accidents. I was right, the family was right, the neighborhood was right, the guys up and down the street were right. 'You're a plum!' my father used to say, meaning, 'Do not fuck up this incomparable American opportunity life has handed you.' Happy at home and happy at school. School was the other home. Chancellor Avenue School on the commercial street running perpendicular to Summit Avenue, three or four minutes from our doorstep, where so much of waking life was spent. My mother was for a few years president of the PTA and therefore knew all my teachers. I was surrounded by a female conspiracy devoted to my safekeeping. I ate up school like it was a smorgasbord, skipping half-grades as I went, which was how I came to be a college freshman at sixteen."

"Writers," I say, "can be sorted into school-lovers and school-haters, I've noticed. None are lukewarm about school."

"School, not home, was where I found out about literature. We owned only four books: three novels by Sir Walter Scott and William L. Shirer's *Berlin Diary*. My mother read bestsellers borrowed at one cent a day from the rental library of our pharmacy. Pearl Buck she adored. Also Louis Bromfield, a truly forgotten name. Nearby was the branch library where the rest of literature patiently waited. I filled my bicycle basket with whatever took my fancy. Adventure stories by Howard Pease. Sagas of early America by Howard Fast, laced with pro-Communist undertones lost on me. Then in high school came the lightning and thunder of Thomas Wolfe. I felt I *was* Eugene Gant, his hero. This was the necessary romanticism of extreme youth."

I wonder whether *Look Homeward, Angel* and *Of Time and the River* were his genesis as a writer.

"Strange to say, I read those without a single thought that I too should write down in deathless lyrical prose the record of my exalted adventures. But I do think the very sensitive, very terrible stories I produced in college must have owed a lot to Wolfe. I remember also some reflections in verse on the falling of the first autumn leaf. I won't be reading any of that juvenilia again to confirm my low opinion of it."

But how did he get from there to the assurance of *Goodbye, Columbus?*

"I improved, though not out of all recognition. As you might expect your dentist to improve.

Goodbye, Columbus is a happy-go-lucky book full of youthful, simple starts that are a vast improvement over the college efforts. In its defense I can say no more than that. Fortunately, I'd been schooled not just by Wolfe but by the Sunday-evening radio comedies: Fibber McGee and Molly, Fred Allen, Jack Benny. Whatever is good in my first book owes something to those masters."

I ask about *Letting Go* and *When She Was Good*, which came next.

"Oh, I wanted to be literary, wanted to be *influenced*. There were Flaubert and Henry James. There were Dreiser and Sherwood Anderson. Under such spells I wrote those two gloomy novels, *Letting Go* and *When She Was Good*, for the second of which I have a soft spot even now. It's got a genuine heroine, Lucy Nelson. But also a one-note depressiveness and no particular color. Some other writer could have written it."

"What follows seems a bolt from the blue."

"I discovered I was not a gloomy but a raucous

talent. And that's the story of *Portnoy's Complaint*, in which I gleefully overthrew my literary education, shed the proprieties to reveal a Jew in all his libidinous tumult—and good taste be damned. People professionally worried about the public image of the Jews were naturally going to be cross. The freewheeling, farcical, ventriloquistic fun Bob Brustein, Al Goldman, Jules Feiffer and I were having at dinner parties—our improvisational theater, you could call it—gave me the idea for a full-scale farce with which to answer the abominations of the time: assassinations, cities afire, the nightly news from Southeast Asia. I flung my harmless obscenities back at the world-historical ones. The book's premise was simple: A young man in psychoanalysis is as trapped in a Jewish joke as was Gregor Samsa in the body of an insect, with lusts as repugnant to his conscience as his conscience is repugnant to his lusts. No wonder he can't stop talking. 'You want to hear everything, Spielvogel? I'm telling you everything.' Did you ever read Bruno Bettelheim's case notes in the voice of Dr. Spielvogel?"

"What?"

"He called it 'Portnoy Psychoanalyzed.' It's what poor beleaguered Spielvogel writes down after the analytic hour is over and Portnoy has mercifully left. He reports that, from time to time, he'd love to reply to his sex-crazed babbler but can't get a word in. Very doleful and funny."

I ask if he knew how seismic the book would be.

"Early chapters excerpted in *Esquire*, *Partisan Review* and *New American Review* created strong commercial expectations and I received a quarter of a million dollars against royalties. A staggering sum back then. I remember taking my parents to lunch to prepare them for what was coming. I said newspaper and magazine and broadcast journalists were likely to contact them and that they should feel free to say thank you for calling and hang up. Years later my father told me that after that lunch my mother burst into tears saying, 'Poor Philip is suffering from delusions of grandeur! He's going to be so terribly let down!' "

I mention that he'd already had a taste of scandal when caught unawares by the response to "Defender of the Faith" when it appeared in *The New Yorker.* The accusation of giving aid and comfort to anti-Semites had stung him terribly. Rabbis in their pulpits had asked what could be done to *silence* such a man.

"Being denounced by the Anti-Defamation League was nothing compared to the firestorm *Portnoy* raised. No less a figure than Professor Gershom Scholem said it was worse than *The Protocols of the Elders of Zion.* The book had too much impact. I was not Norman Mailer. Trouble was not my middle name. The book made me too famous, determined too much of my life to come. People don't believe me when I say this, but I wish I'd just let the individual chapters stand in those magazines. I could have escaped the burden of being a scandal. I could have escaped having my mother in some torment saying, 'Philip, darling, are you—anti-Semitic? Because that's what we hear.'"

Silence, exile, cunning and the three-hour writing rule, Philip used to say of his work ethic. "Same old story. You can't guard a hundred percent. Fifty's a good goal." He on whom the trap of fame had snapped shut when he was thirty-six said the only way forward was to pay no attention. "The writer," he told me, "wants intelligent recognition. Not to be disappointed, let down—insulted. And what if he gets recognition? There's always the source of disappointment lurking somewhere. Which means everywhere."

A winter's evening in the early naughts: "I must warn you, Ben. You've got a face that shows too much." Though the conversation was fluent, we didn't know each other very well yet. "I eat in dumps," he'd told me. It was true. That night's venue was an undistinguished Italian restaurant in his neighborhood. I'll simply call it, as he did, The Meatball. When Philip was depressed he'd want to go there. I quickly learned to recognize any proposal to dine at The Meatball as an SOS. Perhaps the "too much" showing on my face that night was worry.

The problem was that he was waging love on two fronts at once. Or was it three? A natural bachelor, as I say. More frankly, a law unto himself. "No punishment is too harsh," he told me, "for the demiurge who thought up fidelity." That Philip was both an ardent lover and a sexual anarch was the inner dynamism of his life as well as his art. "Monogamy would not have been in me had I lived in the era of Cotton Mather. As it was, I lived in the era of *Screw* magazine and Linda Lovelace."

But if monogamy was anathema to him so was enduring the opprobrium the polyamorous suffer. In *My Life as a Man* the hero, Peter Tarnopol, speaks for his maker when he says: "I may not be well suited for the notoriety that attends the publication of an unabashed and unexpurgated history of one's erotic endeavors. As the history itself will testify, I happen to be no more immune to shame or built for public exposure than the next burgher with shades on his bedroom windows and a latch on the bathroom door—indeed, maybe what the whole history signifies is that I am sensitive to nothing in all the world as I am to my moral reputation."

Torment about rectitude plagued him as acutely as any itch in the loins. That a man who'd written those books and led that life should be so primly worried about what people were saying struck me as funny. It may, from time to time, have been amusement at his expense that was registering on my face.

"Philip, I'm going to introduce you to a better class of restaurant."

As a novelist, he believed that the truth was compounded of perspectives and partial understandings. After the early books he shunned omniscience.

"The fact remains that getting people right is not what living is all about anyway," he writes in *American Pastoral.* "It's getting them wrong that is living, getting them wrong and wrong and wrong and then, on careful reconsideration, getting them wrong again. That's how we know we're alive: we're wrong." And in *Sabbath's Theater*: "If what you think happened happens to not ever match up with what somebody else thinks happened, how could you say you know even that? Everybody got everything wrong."

Yet he was not similarly skeptical about his own self-understanding in real life—"the unwritten world," as he preferred to call it. Bluntly, Philip was allergic to the idea that he could have been at fault in either of his unhappy marriages and to the idea that the party of the other part might, in both cases, have had grievances worth considering. His own angle of vision was complete and unfailing. Other accounts were distortions. This explains so much about him: for example, his vexed search for a biographer, which dragged on for years. He was looking not for a Boswell to fix him to the page but for a ventriloquist's dummy to sit in his lap. It was really an impossible quest. He wanted someone first-rate he could entirely bend to his point of view. What he got in Blake Bailey, the eventual official biographer, was someone more independent-minded, indeed more formidable, than Philip could calmly resign himself to. "Two things await me," he used to say, "death and my biographer. I don't know which is more to be feared."

About Mary McCarthy he said: "She had a very strong need to be right."

"You too?"

"To *prevail.*"

It was certainly true that he never grew dispassionate about injuries from the past, or about the splendid sufficiency of his own point of view on them. In any conflict he needed, in the telling, to have morally prevailed. At another of our early dinners (in a restaurant of my choosing) he told me, as he sooner or later told everyone, the lurid tale of his first marriage. It was always a matter of evening the score with the late Margaret Martinson Williams Roth, a divorced mother of two when he met her, whose children the courts rotated among relatives. Little could I have known on this first hearing that I'd listen to the story a hundred times more. Despite her death she needed further—no, endless—pulverization.

They had married early in 1959 after she faked the results of a pregnancy test by paying a pregnant woman in Tompkins Square Park to furnish the urine sample. "*Her* art of fiction," as Tarnopol says of Maggie's counterpart, Maureen. " 'Creativity' gone awry." She'd already threatened suicide. Guilty-hearted good boy, believing the hoax, Philip accepted her umpteenth proposal of marriage.

"We'll be happy as kings!" Maggie crowed, just

as Maureen does in *My Life as a Man*, and declared that as Mrs. Roth she'd be more than willing to have an abortion. Which she, who hadn't been pregnant in the first place, promptly went off and pretended to do. She spent the afternoon in a Times Square movie house watching two features of Susan Hayward in *I Want to Live!*, then came home to East Tenth Street, disheveled and reporting on how horrible the supposed ordeal had been, and put herself to bed.

Such were the two lies upon which their marriage was founded. It would not be dissolved till her death ten years later in a car crash on one of the transverses of Central Park.

That evening at dinner I jumped in my chair when Philip banged his hand on the table—banged as if Maggie's deceptions had happened last month, not most of a lifetime ago. "I found out the whole outlandish truth when she confessed it following her suicide attempt in 1962. The dedicatee of *Letting Go* and model for Martha Reganhart"—the novel's

scrappy, lively heroine and best thing in the book—
"was nemesis itself and the vandal of my young
manhood. The goal thereafter was never to be
hoodwinked again."

"How about leaving her to heaven, Philip?"

But he couldn't. "A writer needs to be driven
round the bend," he told me. "Needs his poisons.
He battens on them." The death of one or the other
party was, Philip felt, the only possible conclusion
to their unholy union. But he knew he owed her.
"Without doubt she was my worst enemy ever," he
writes in *The Facts*, "but, alas, she was also nothing
less than the greatest creative writing teacher of
them all, specialist par excellence in the aesthetics
of extremist fiction."

Then, suddenly, she was dead. "All I had done
the night before was to close my eyes and go to
sleep, and now everything was over." When on that
May morning in 1968 the news of the fatal wreck
came, he believed it a sinister ploy cooked up by her
lawyer to get him to say something usable in court.

The convenience of her death seemed too glaring a deus ex machina, more peremptory even than the death of Lucy Nelson in *When She Was Good*, his novel from a year earlier, whose heroine is likewise based on Maggie and whose death is eerily predictive of hers. "Every writer," he told me more than once, "has the experience of imagining things that then come to pass. But my tormented heroine's violent death one year before Maggie's seemed too, too—"

"Too on the nose, as the young say?"

"Too on the nose."

After her funeral, Philip went to what may or may not have been the spot where she died, lifted his face to the clement sun and rejoiced in his improbable freedom.

That we owe a lot to our misadventures is a key to his books. In *My Life as a Man*—that "autofiction," to use the fashionable term, of the years with Maggie—there's a poet in residence at Quahsay, the Yaddo-like artists' colony to which Peter

Tarnopol has retreated, who drinks everything on the premises, including the vanilla extract, before being carted off to AA. "Ah, don't worry," she calls from the departing car, "if it wasn't for my mistakes I'd still be back on the front porch in Boise."

First Martha Reganhart. Then Lucy Nelson. Then Maureen Tarnopol. Maggie had been a powerful spur to Philip's artistry. She and her family were his education in the small-town ghastliness on which American naturalism has prospered: penury, domestic violence, alcoholism, teenage pregnancy, incarceration. The perky square-jawed blonde whom the University of Chicago instructor in the glen-plaid suit had so blithely engaged in conversation in the doorway of a Fifty-Seventh Street bookshop seemed a veteran of harder knocks than the Weequahic section could provide knowledge of. She was real life, the deep America. Theodore Dreiser and Sherwood Anderson would have agreed. But they would not have mistaken her for harmless. She was

Philip's bighearted mistake. He never calmed down about their connubial hell. He still felt the heat of it. "Good Intentions Paving Company!" he'd sometimes pick up the phone and say—in old age, when all but medical battles were behind him.

To put a little something on Maggie's side of the scale, one might observe that she liked being lied to no better than other wives do. Good though his *intentions* were, Philip had to roam. And fib about it. "Every knuckle dragger's an Olivier," he used to say, "when required to deceive his wife. The wisdom of it is cumulative, handed down through the generations."

"Through the generations? You think your father strayed?"

"No, no. But in the fullness of time he had sons to atone for his monogamy." Yet Philip made a poor Don Juan. He was too apt to fall in love. Then, having fallen in love, he needed to escape from the presumed monogamy love entailed, needed to fall in love again. This was a lifelong pattern and furnishes reason to regard Maggie, as I say, a bit more sympathetically than Roth loyalists do. Of course she was driven to jealous stratagems—Philip was undomesticatable. She raged with cause, turning up at his classroom to berate him and worse. She was a street fighter from nowhere possessed of a marital ideal with which her husband did not concur. The unholiness of their bond had as much to do with his profligacy as her possessiveness. His determination to make himself the nice-boy victim of a Medea or a Hedda Gabler or some other succubus remains hard to credit. She felt betrayed early and often. (One evening over dinner I used the term "philanderer." "We're all better off without that word," he snapped. It may have been his least favorite in the language. Whereas the word he loved best from childhood was "away.")

Driving from Italy to France with her during the infernal Guggenheim year of 1959, Philip had nearly lost control of their car on a steep road when Maggie grabbed the wheel. Some other woman was the likely cause of the argument; other women were what she was always in a rage about. Philip hypothesized that the man who was with her that night in Central Park was getting the same treatment at the wheel. He suffered a minor head injury, she a fatal one. "My emancipator," Philip called him.

250 Melius Road, Warren, Connecticut

CHAPTER FOUR

HOUSEKEEPING IN AMERICA

It is 2008 or 2009, a crisp autumn day. We've gone for a walk in Theodore Roosevelt Park behind the Museum of Natural History. A monument with the names of America's Nobel laureates has been erected here, perhaps a thousand yards from Philip's doorstep. As we examine the monument, a gnarled woman approaches. "Looking for your name? It's not there!" she says to him and darts off like a shot.

The Nobel drama became increasingly tedious as the years wore on. Each October came the rumor: He was tipped to win. Ladbrokes had him at three to one. A couple of times he even defied fate by saying he'd cover my expenses to Stockholm. We tried to talk about other things. Then, after the disappointing announcement, I'd recite the honor roll of those overlooked: Henry James, Tolstoy, Proust, others. But it gnawed Philip to be denied that particular laurel. He took to calling it the Anybody-But-Roth Prize. October was the cruelest month.

Your path has been your own," he told me, which meant a great deal or nothing at all. I decided on the former. He liked the vigorous attitudes I brought to my life. "You've found a good mean— equal disdain for boasting and false modesty." He called me a homemade cosmopolitan, the nicest compliment I've ever received. After my brother's sudden death in a snowmobiling accident in 2006, he phoned every day for weeks, then months. He'd say: "It eases my mind to hear you." When at last I could laugh again he said: "That's what I've been waiting for." He was the chosen parent of my middle age. Ours was an elective genealogy, "a genealogy that isn't genetic," as he calls it in *I Married a Communist*—leading to the orphanhood that is total, "when you're out there in this thing all alone."

Philip's inner life was gargantuan. Insatiable emotional appetites—for rage as for love—led into paths where he seethed with loathing or desire. "There's too much of you, Philip. All your emotions are outsize."

"I've written in order not to die of them." To be stuck with the untransformed unforeseen, all the terrible contingencies, "sans language, shape, structure, meaning—sans the unities, the catharsis," as he puts it in *The Human Stain*, would have burned him up.

He never stopped marveling at how *contingently* a fate is made. It was, for him, what was most basic to storytelling: the happenstance that, in retrospect, turns epic. The owl of Minerva takes flight and all that might not have been becomes all that has incontrovertibly happened, a shimmering thread the Fates wove.

We're attending Russ Murdoch's annual pig roast near Philip's house in Warren. The sight of the cooked animal—nose, eyeballs, hooves, corkscrew tail—turns my legs to jelly.

"You look peaked," Philip says. "Go sit down. With your back to the beast. I'll bring you a little of that potato salad."

I shake my head, put a hand to my mouth, puff out my cheeks.

"Maybe just some carbonated water?"

I nod weakly.

"Breathe through your mouth," he advises, exactly as my old man would have done. Probably his too. We've made a list of fatherisms: "Buckle down, Winsocki." "Like it or lump it." "You're pressing your luck." "Who do you think we are, the Rockefellers?" "You're going to put out an eye with that thing." "Don't get your bowels in an uproar." "I'll take it up with General MacArthur." "Ask your mother." "I've been very patient with you." "Can I make it any clearer?" "You're on thin ice." "You've got more hours in that bathroom than Rickenbacker had in the air." "You'll be saying you're sorry in a minute." "Don't make a federal case out of it." By way of encouragement: "Keep your pecker up." In response to a request for extra money: "Soon as my rich uncle gets off the poor farm." When a new appliance was being assembled: "Don't *force* it!" Sometimes just "Sez you" or "Malarky." Sometimes, and unanswerably: "Get with the program."

"My father," I said, "would announce, when consuming any spicy dish: 'This is as hot as Aunt Blanche!' My brother and I begged to know more about her and this led to quite a saga. She'd been the madam of a joy house in New Orleans and after that a United States senator. One day soon she'd be swooping down to pay us a visit in Fort Worth. I pictured a Mae West type filling up the living room and wondered just how hot Aunt Blanche was."

"Were you a puzzle to him?"

"He wondered how he'd engendered me, yes. I remember the look on his face when he asked who'd won the softball game and I told him I thought it had been a tie. The most scathing fatherism at our house was chagrined silence after a remark of mine like that."

"Herman's best fatherisms were authoritatively delivered pearls of wisdom based on fragmentary or dubious information. I remember V-J Day at Bradley Beach: the huzzahs and tears and a conga line forming up on the boardwalk. And Dad saying, 'From here on, boys, we're going *atomic!*'"

The only real opponent Philip faced in young manhood was his father, and it was opposition of the most loving kind. Herman feared the larger world, feared what it could do to his wide-eyed, unwary boys. He particularly feared what sex could do to them. I don't think there were more than a dozen real quarrels under that roof, the majority of them having to do with Philip's need for independence. The Roths were a sparkling example of what family life could be: the American dream coming true. The ballast was right. The happy childhood Philip wrote of had not been manufactured ex post facto. It was real. Accidental but real.

As for his mother, he reports in *Patrimony* that Bess Roth single-handedly established "a first-class domestic-management and mothering company back in 1927," the year of Sandy's birth, raising "housekeeping in America to a great art."

Cut to manhood:

Dr. Hans Joachim Kleinschmidt, the Prussian-born psychoanalyst who fled Hitler in 1933 and was Philip's doctor in the sixties (and the prototype of Dr. Spielvogel in two of his novels), decided that an unacknowledged hatred and fear of The Phallic Threatening Mother was what was unconsciously eating his patient. "There in a nutshell," said Philip, "is what's wrong with their whole five-and-dime pseudoscience—a belief that each of us, Roth and every other schnook, is stamped with the same story. No doubt Freud was a gifted mythmaker.

Problem is, that's what his theories amount to—myths. Psychoanalysis is procrustean and boring. But I was as big a sucker for it as the rest of my generation. Did you know Kleinschmidt immortalized me in a paper called 'The Angry Act: The Role of Aggression in Creativity'? His earthshaking conclusion? That I suffered from—you guessed it—castration anxiety at the hands of my terrifying mother. I told him that was baloney. He told me I was blocking."

Bess, that least terrifying of mothers (in truth it was Philip who terrified her), died suddenly at seventy-seven. She and Herman had gone with friends for a seafood supper. She ordered New England clam chowder. Herman got Manhattan-style. When their orders came Bess said, "I don't want this soup." Herman said, "Take mine—we'll switch." But she was gone.

Philip and I had the same family configuration: mother, father, two sons. Like him, I idolized my older brother. Like him, I was the younger by some years. Musically speaking, our brothers had been the theme and we were the variation.

Like Philip, I'd tagged along. "If Sandy stopped short, my nose would go up his ass." Sandy had been an artist from childhood and in high school would come to New York on Saturdays to study at the Art Students League on West Fifty-Seventh Street. He was the artist in the family. As a twelve-year-old, Philip would sit wonder-struck as Sandy recounted drawing naked women in Manhattan. "He was the pathfinder. He came home and described for me the origin of the world and everything else he'd seen." It was Sandy who brought from Pratt Institute, to which he'd also gone, a list of books with the heading SUMMER READING! Philip took it to the Weequahic branch library and pulled down the recommended volumes: *Main Street*, *A Farewell to Arms*, *Winesburg, Ohio*. Curiosity germinated.

"Sandy was handsome and dashing, I see by the photos."

"Handsome, yes. The handsomest kid in the neighborhood. But dashing? Not at all. I could never understand it, but he was *awkward* with girls. It was left to less-handsome me to excel where big brother had faltered. I was the heartthrob. Also the better athlete. And I was the one who, in adulthood, claimed the artistic vocation. For all his gifts, once he was a husband and father, Sandy devolved into a weekend painter. The advertising business had claimed him."

"How'd he feel about you? Did he feel usurped?"

"So much of what he was feeling I never knew. I knew I loved him. I knew he endured me. Had I usurped him? I think I tried his patience. He used to tell people he'd kill me if I wrote about him. But I'm still here, as you see."

I was with Philip in Chicago when Sandy died in May of 2009 after long struggles with heart disease, prostate cancer and osteoporosis. He told me more than once that the six-foot-three brother had lost six inches of height to the bone illness. Philip remained outwardly composed but told stories all week about Sandy. He and his first wife, Trudy, had adopted two sons. It was Philip who met with the birth mother of Seth, the elder of the two boys, and took the newborn to Sandy and Trudy. He mentioned how Sandy could not stand classical music—"longhair music," he called it—and formed the radical opinion that no one actually could, that we Bach, Beethoven and Brahms lovers were just putting on the dog. Philip recalled also the three of them, Sandy and sons, a few weeks after Trudy's death, closing themselves into one of the bedrooms of the house in Warren and sobbing loudly, given up to the lamentation they'd been holding in. It was the most wicked of earworms, children in anguish, and Philip could not get it out of his head.

Every house has its particular smell, its particular sounds. Philip's country place is a three-story clapboard whose core dates to the first administration of George Washington. The native fragrance is of its ancient pine floorboards, which moan pleasantly underfoot. So do the graceful front stairs and too-steep back stairs. Low doorways, irregular rooms: all so Yankee. The house is situated on a hundred fifty acres known in the olden day as Flat Rock Farm. A couple hundred yards from the handsome old structure is a two-room studio—obviously the inspiration for Nathan Zuckerman's spartan retreat in the Berkshires. (Unlike his maker, Nathan lives simply. Unlike his novel-writing protagonist, Philip lives well.) Beyond the house and low stone walls are fields of Indian paintbrush, goldenrod, Queen Anne's lace. Beyond the fields are impenetrable woodlands in which woodpeckers joyously peck. Warblers crisscross the summer air. A heron angles into the marsh across the road. The locusts are ringing and the Appalachian Trail is nearby. Bear leave their calling cards as close as the doorstep and Philip keeps a large ivory-handled bell in the foyer with which to scare them off before venturing out after dark.

"Philip, I've never seen these bears you talk about."

"But they've seen you."

So pastoral is the refuge that we sometimes disagree about what day of the week it is. Tonight peepers are singing in the marsh. Reluctantly, Philip has agreed to watch *Now, Voyager,* a favorite of mine. That week, my attempts to interest him in the films of Douglas Sirk had run aground. We got no further than the overheated credits to *Written on the Wind.*

"What do you see in all this Hollywood dreck, Ben? Really, I want to know." His own tastes run to Kurosawa and Satyajit Ray and Fellini. "And why are you gay men so beguiled by Bette Davis? You don't look twice at Ava Gardner, who was, *to put it mildly*, more attractive. She had an enduring sexiness, even in London. In the eighties. When I had her." (I tell you this, reader, in strict confidence—as it was told to me.)

"Ava's a special taste, Philip. Bette's universal. Bitchery and noblesse alternate from picture to picture. In this one she's all New England conscience and stiff upper lip. In others, no squalor is beneath her. As Regina in *The Little Foxes* her face is painted a ghoulish white. Ever see *Jezebel* or *In This Our Life?* Bloodcurdling. Whereas beautiful Ava was just beautiful Ava."

"Ava used to say, 'People are always claiming Elizabeth Taylor was beautiful. Untrue! Elizabeth Taylor was pretty. *I* was beautiful.'"

For the first half of *Now, Voyager* Philip makes cracks about Bette, then grows quiet. Is the movie setting its hooks for him? "I get it," he says at the finish. "The unspoken part is that she and Paul Henreid have had sex down in Rio and now must pay for it with a lifetime of abstinence. But that will be noble, fine and pure. 'Jerry, don't let's ask for the moon. We have the stars!' Phooey, Ben."

"Oh, I think you liked it, and her, better than you admit." Next evening I propose *Dark Victory*.

"Not on your life."

"All right then. *The Barefoot Contessa.*"

"Not a chance. Tonight we're seeing *Pather Panchali*. Tomorrow's *Aparajito*. Sunday night is *Apur Sansar*."

So we sit down to our weekend of Ray's trilogy.

"This leaves your *chazzerai*"—Yiddish for pigswill—"in the dust," he says at the breathtaking conclusion of *Pather Panchali*. Apu's father raises a cache of pages and says, smiling in his tears: "All my plans came to nothing. I wanted to be a writer. Look at my manuscripts, eaten by worms. I wanted to educate my boy. That came to nothing. And my little girl slipped away." The last thing you see is a snake entering the house he and his family have abandoned.

"Want to know the difference between *Now, Voyager* and *Pather Panchali*? It's melodrama versus drama, coercion of emotion versus elicitation of emotion." He's right, of course, but I could happily return to thirties Hollywood on Saturday evening.

Instead, dinner completed and the dishwasher humming, we have the demanding *Aparajito* with its Benares sequences and further untimely deaths. Then, on Sunday, *Apur Sansar*, surely the masterpiece of the three.

"What the whole thing adds up to is a *Bildungsroman*, the coming into his own of Apu," says Philip, waxing pedagogical. "A *Bildungsroman* in which loss is the teacher. Sister, father, mother, wife. Life has denuded Apu. As for worldly ambitions, those go too. He's a literary flop like his father before him. He casts his probably awful novel to the winds. This is, you'll pardon my saying so, a bit stronger than 'Don't let's ask for the moon, Jerry.'"

There was, too, his love of Bergman. He recalled a chance meeting with Hannah Arendt in which he said, "I've just seen the most wonderful picture, Miss Arendt—*Cries and Whispers*." She fitted a cigarette into a tortoiseshell holder and gave him an appraising look. "Scandinavian kitsch!" she said and walked off.

"I hadn't been able to take my eyes off her upper lip. It quivered expressively and seemed the precise location of her genius. I knew she could see how scared I was." Now the two of them, Hannah and Philip, lie some feet apart in the Bard College Cemetery and will have all the time they need to compose their differences.

———•———

CHAPTER FIVE

THERE IS A GOD AND HIS NAME IS LAUGHTER

Knowing of my particular love for his 1993 novel *Operation Shylock*, Philip gave me for my sixty-third birthday about eighty handwritten worksheets from an early draft, along with a facetious cover letter from Meema Gitcha, his paternal grandmother's sister and a character in the book.

Going to Meema Gitcha's house in Connecticut seemed to him as a boy like going back to the Old Country itself. "A five-hour car ride in those days. Aunts, uncles, cousins, my grandmother, all packed in together, coming and going. It was somehow the most Jewishy-Yiddishy event of my childhood—we could have been driving all the way back to the folkland of Galicia traveling up to Danbury on those trips." There was a lot of melancholy in Meema Gitcha's house, a lot of illness waiting in the wings—a lot of pessimistic expectation. Of car wrecks, for instance. When they got back to Newark they always phoned to confirm that they hadn't been wiped out on the road home. A signal had been arranged. They'd call person-to-person and ask for one Moishe Pipik. And Gitcha would reply: "Moishe Pipik? He's not here! He left half an hour ago!" and bang down the receiver.

So many of the best American novelists sooner or later produce a work that is extreme by the standards of its siblings, a novel that seems crazy vis-à-vis the rest of the author's work: Melville's *Pierre*, for instance, or James's *The Golden Bowl*; Faulkner's *Absalom, Absalom!* qualifies, as does Nathanael West's *Miss Lonelyhearts*. And Flannery O'Connor's *The Violent Bear It Away*. Bellow's *Henderson the Rain King* qualifies. Cheever's *Bullet Park* richly qualifies, as do Stanley Elkin's *The Living End* and William H. Gass's *The*

Tunnel. In each of these, the writer seems to have decided that too much is too little, that too far is not far
enough, that it is time to go for more than broke.

These books haven't a thing in common except
that they're American—could only be American—
and that they're 100 percent weird. *Operation Shylock* joins this august and *meshuggah* club. In it the
author achieves a genuinely Kafkan (which is to
say, indecipherable) parable, whose grotesque
premise is this: An identity thief calling himself
Philip Roth, and identical to Philip Roth in appear-
ance, manner, speech, dress, grooming, you name
it, goes around Israel saying things that make the
anti-Zionism of Noam Chomsky sound like a UJA
pitch. This impostor's creed goes by the name of
Diasporism and has as its major tenet that the Ashkenazim of Israel should go back to the countries
they came from—where, the false Roth argues,
they'll be greeted with hosannahs. Just imagine
those tearful, joyous scenes of welcome in the
streets of Riga, Vilnius, Warsaw, Kraków,

Bucharest, Kiev, Salonica, et cetera. Hooray, hooray, our Jews have come home!

And here is how the real Roth replies to his dim-bulb double: "I lived eleven years in London—not in bigoted, backwater, pope-ridden Poland but in civilized, secularized, worldly-wise England. When the first hundred thousand Jews come rolling into Waterloo Station with all their belongings in tow, I really want to be there. Invite me, won't you? When the first hundred thousand Diasporist evacuees voluntarily surrender their criminal Zionist homeland to the suffering Palestinians and disembark on England's green and pleasant land, I want to see with my very own eyes the welcoming committee of English goyim waiting on the platform with their champagne. 'They're here! More Jews! Jolly good!'"

In order to cope with the lunacy of the provocation, Roth the Real gives this mirror-image nemesis—this ideologizing nudnik, this undergroundling, this Philip Roth minus intellect, wit, artistry, this would-be secret-sharer—a deflationary nickname: Moishe Pipik, the Roths' and Meema Gitcha's old code word. "The derogatory, joking nonsense name that translates literally to Moses Bellybutton and that probably connoted something slightly different to every Jewish family on our block—the little guy who wants to be a big shot, the kid who pisses in his pants, the someone who is a bit ridiculous, a bit funny, a bit childish, the comical shadow alongside whom we had all grown up."

What this realization, that his antagonist is a Moishe Pipik, grants Philip is the indemnification of laughter. Heinrich Heine once said that there is a God and his name is Aristophanes. In other words, there is a God and his name is Laughter. And while you laugh, you surmount life's contradictions, take flight even as the joke-proof all around you wonder what's so funny. Philip writes: "I felt what I'd felt way, way back when, because of the happenstance of a lucky childhood, I didn't know I could be overcome by anything—all the endowment that was originally mine before I was ever impeded by guilt, a full human being strong in the magic." Philip says that if it were Aristophanes rather than Yahweh that the Jews worship, he'd be in schul three times a day.

These protections of laughter—sudden, unbidden, delicious, fleeting—are for him a magic ticket back to the vanished world of the early familiar, the lost Eden of the Weequahic section, Newark, New Jersey. At the center of *Operation Shylock* the author says: "I left the front stoop on Leslie Street, ate of the fruit of the tree of fiction, and nothing, neither reality nor myself, had been the same since." It is laughter and only laughter that for a moment restores the lost simplicity, certifies that it was once real—life unriven by anything insoluble, the past paradise whose memento is present laughter.

I find here the red thread in Philip's work, the particular thing called "Rothian": Alongside the tough-mindedness of the man's way forward—through independence, sex, love, hatred, doubt, creativity, understanding, bewilderment, guilt, shame, fear, grief—alongside this well-known

tough-mindedness there is the Rothian tender-
heartedness, the momentary way back out of all
complexity, back to when he'd just been Bess and
Herman's boy, not yet also Franz Kafka's and Fyodor
Dostoyevsky's and Louis-Ferdinand Céline's boy
too. Before he'd taken upon himself the burden
of disclosing life through the medium of language; of revealing the fates of irreducibly particular persons, both everything that is on the outside
and everything within that passeth show; of making novels, bright books of life in which sometimes, as in *Shylock*, life looks least like what it is
supposed to look like in order that it may be most
like whatever it is. Is not a portion of what is truest
in fiction owing to this more-than-realist bent
(think of Gogol's "The Nose," Kafka's *The Metamorphosis*, Dostoyevsky's *The Double*), this appetite
for the improbable or impossible made persuasive,
this lifelikeness in a funhouse mirror, this depar-
ture from verisimilitude for the sake of a fiercer
mimesis?

A renowned comedian, formerly thought funny, lives in my building. Philip is intrigued by this figure, whom he calls an anti-Semite's delight, and is forever pumping me for information about him.

I phone late.

"Was hoping you'd call."

I tell him You-Know-Who has sprung for a new toupee, a brilliant red one. When he sees you he says, "Hello, hello," his laugh line of yesteryear. He thinks it's a scream. Late nights he lurks in the lobby, adjusting his rug in the mirror—he's *vain* about it—while awaiting a car to deliver him to the night's pleasures. "He's got a harem of prostitutes he calls 'my *schvartzes*,' lovingly. The man is an open sewer."

"Who's his pimp?"

I report that he uses several. I've seen him out front with a variety of sketchy characters.

"He nicely makes my point about the Jews: They are neither worse nor better than other people.

Therefore neither anti- nor philo-Semite be. Email me tomorrow, Ben. At my email address up here in the country."

I say that we've been through that already. That email addresses aren't location-specific. Your email is in the ether, not at any street address. He hangs up without goodbye, as so often. When was this? Around 2012? Soon enough he was reading *iPhone for Dummies* and getting abreast of the new technology.

By the time I knew him, Philip hated the stage and would, like Cromwell, have shut down all theaters if he could. "People up there pretending to be who they're not. People in the audience pretending to believe the pretense."

"Strange attitude for a fiction writer. So many have wanted to write plays too."

"And broke their hearts trying. Henry James.

Saul. And *me*, the worst playwright in American history."

He did like my theater chronicles though:

"You still awake?" I was just home from a revival of *A View from the Bridge*.

"Tell all."

"There seems to be no end to these new productions of Miller. It was awful, but something redeeming happened in act two. Something in the audience, where the drama was as considerable as that on stage. At the crucial moment when Rodolfo takes off his shirt to reveal a Herculean torso, someone three rows ahead of me slumped into the aisle. Fainted dead away. The show went on, but all eyes were riveted to row six where a flurry of ushers had converged."

"They revived her?"

"*Him*, Philip! These are modern times. I might have swooned myself."

On another evening, he particularly wanted me to report on a downtown production of *Waiting for*

Godot, in Yiddish with English supertitles. The whole thing was on a shoestring and beautiful and made perfect sense: Vladimir and Estragon dragging themselves through a blasted, barbarized landscape, beseeching life for a meaning, declaring that there's nothing to be done—"Gornisht tsu ton."

"The audience was what you would expect—elderly Jewish intellectuals and a smattering of *Hasidim*. And next to me a superbly dressed young black couple, emissaries from the realm of the good looking. About fifteen minutes in, the young woman begins to rustle, then opens her handbag for an inventory, then loudly sighs. 'Lamir gyn,' says Vladimir. 'Mir kenen nisht,' explains Estragon. 'Far vos nisht?' asks Vladimir. 'Mir vartn far Godot,' explains Estragon. The young man leans to his lady and whispers: 'Baby, somebody stiffed me with some really bad tickets.' At intermission they flee, taking all glamour with them."

"Ben, you can't imagine how much better this is than actual theatergoing."

As a high-spirited thirtysomething, Philip wrote *Portnoy's Complaint* "to let the whole creature out." It's a young man's book. "An overflowing libido is appealing in a young man," he used to say, "nervous-making in a middle-aged man, comical in an old man." Or tragicomic, as in *Sabbath's Theater*, that immaculate intertwining of filth and beauty, his hymn of praise to the sex drive out of season. Reading it at my local coffee shop a day or two after Michiko Kakutani's indignant review, I was approached by a *Times* reader who said: "That book is obscene."

"Glad you get the point, lady."

Kakutani, with whom Philip already had considerable unhappy history, appears in the novel as a villainess variously named Kuziduzi, Kakizomi, Kakizaki and the Japanese Viperina. You wonder, given these protean appearances in the novel, that she hadn't seen fit to recuse herself from reviewing it.

Sabbath is indeed a wantonly dirty book, an

unprecedented provocation. Pornographers, despair! Roth has seen and raised you. Before going on to the historical chronicles of his last phase—*American Pastoral, I Married a Communist, The Human Stain, The Plot Against America*—Philip had to flow as humbly as the gutters. He writes of his antinomian hero Mickey Sabbath: "Yes, yes, yes he felt uncontrollable tenderness for his own shit-filled life. And a laughable hunger for more. More defeat! More disappointment! More deceit! More loneliness! More arthritis! . . . God willing, more cunt! More disastrous entanglement in everything. For a pure sense of being tumultuously alive, you can't beat the nasty side of existence."

When writing the novel he'd tell himself: "Let the repellent in. Extenuate nothing." When finished he could say with Melville that he'd written a wicked book and felt spotless as the lamb. The novel's undertow really has nothing to do with "the urge to spurt that maketh monkeys of us all." It has to do with Mickey's unassuageable grief for Morty, his elder brother shot down over the Philippines in the last year of the war; for their mother who declines and dies of the loss; for a first wife who has vanished into thin air; for Drenka Balich, his lover and mortally ill sex-teacher.

"I've needed sex," Philip told me, "in order to be indomitable, briefly deathless. The admitted filth of *Sabbath's Theater* was my weapon, as a writer, in unequal combat with the basic mortal facts. Drenka is profligacy itself, sexual joy itself. She is also riddled with cancer. Mere sex is hardly what the book's about. You want mere sex? Read lesser Roth—say, *Portnoy's Complaint*, that romp, that testament of youth. *Sabbath's Theater* is death and grief all the way down, the answer my maturity gave back to *Portnoy*. My grown-up—grown-old—purpose was to violate every canon of seemliness and good taste, to affront and affront till there was no one left to affront. I seem to have succeeded. The book has proved to be an equal-opportunity offender." It even produced an anonymous threat on Philip's life.

(What drove the would-be assassin? Had he read Kakutani's review?)

Sabbath is about nothing keeping its promise. Mickey's profligacy is his rejoinder to the accumulating losses: "We are immoderate because grief is immoderate, all the hundreds and thousands of kinds of grief."

What's perhaps strongest in that very strong book is the scene where Mickey tells Drenka about swimming at the Jersey shore when he was a boy: "Sand scratching your eyes, stuffing your ears, packing the crotch of your suit . . . and then, spurred by a sudden heroic impulse, spinning about onto your belly for the dive to the ocean floor. Sixteen, eighteen, twenty feet down. *Where's the bottom?* Then the lung-bursting battle up to the oxygen with a fistful of sand to show Morty."

It is my favorite thing in all Philip's thirty-one books. Whatever else his antihero is, at that moment Sabbath is the American Sublime. Asked what he would do if nihilistic Mickey came through the door of his shipshape, no-pin-out-of-place apartment, Philip answered: "Throw him out. Anybody would. Too dirty. I'd throw him out." But with a benediction.

Ben, tell about your heterosexual adventures," he says. Does he imagine I've such a deep shelf of them to draw from?

"Tell about your homosexual adventures, Philip."

"I asked you first."

"On New Year's Eve of 1972, I had my one and only heterosexual adventure."

"Lucky girl."

"In a motel room. In Fort Worth. She was beautiful and full of charm. And deserved better than to ring in the New Year with someone who found her as arousing as a cigar-store Indian. Now you."

"My *best* homosexual adventure? It happened at

a rest stop. I was taking a leak in the men's room when a fellow popped up beside me and said in a whisper, 'Can I blow you?' 'No,' I whispered back, then remembered my manners. 'But thanks!' I called over my shoulder as he fled."

"That's not a homosexual adventure, Philip."

We are on our way to New York-Presbyterian, as so often, for tests. Philip is in pain. I hail a cab at the corner of Amsterdam and Seventy-Ninth. Our driver has Rush Limbaugh bloviating at high volume on the radio and is aggressively flatulent.

Philip turns to me, his face a study. "Are we to be spared nothing?" he asks.

Philip, Henry James says adjectives are the sugar of literature and adverbs the salt. What the devil does he mean by that?"

"That too much of either spoils the dish."

It is summer again. We are again so bucolic as to have trouble remembering what day of the week it is. I am reading *The Golden Bowl*.

"Trying to get the bad taste of Mickey out of your mouth?"

"Just trying to see if I can still get through things this hard. Book's too rich for my blood—"

"For anyone's."

"—but I'm reading it anyhow."

Meanwhile, I've christened as our golden bowl the earthenware vessel in which salad gets tossed at the kitchen table here each evening.

"Doesn't Fanny Assingham smash it on the hearth?" Philip asks.

"Exactly."

"Remind me why she does that."

In the bughouse

"The bowl is flawed. It's got a crack in the crystal under the gilding. And it becomes, by an ingenious plot device, the proof that Charlotte Stant and the Prince have been lovers. Seeing the bowl in the shop of a Bloomsbury antiquarian, Charlotte had wanted to give it to Amerigo as a gift. He'd spotted the crack and said it was unlucky to possess such a thing. Then, years later, Maggie has innocently bought it for her father and been told by the shopkeeper of the lovers who'd almost purchased the bowl but changed their minds. It becomes apparent to her in a flash that the lovers in the Bloomsbury shop were Amerigo and Charlotte."

"But why does Fanny smash it?"

"I think it's something James scholars argue about. A desperate attempt to destroy evidence? But it has the opposite effect, corroborating Maggie's suspicion. What fewer readers remember is that Maggie bends down to collect the fragments. She'll mend the bowl—as she will her marriage, shattered by adultery."

"Fanny deserves her name, as I remember," Philip says, and likens her to an enemy of his, the writer Francine du Plessix Gray, his neighbor in Warren: "Endless meddling, grandiose motives." Philip died convinced that Francine had written a poison-pen note he received ("Everyone knows you're having an affair with" et cetera), which later, transformed, furnished a delectable plot point in *The Human Stain.* He had on his side a handwriting expert who compared the note to other samples of Francine's ropy scrawl. Philip believed as well that she'd ghostwritten, under deep cover, *Leaving a Doll's House,* Claire Bloom's memoir of her life with and marriage to Philip.

He evened the score with Gray in a series of satirical portraits, including someone named Countess du Plissitas in *Sabbath's Theater.* In *I Married a Communist* he more than got even with Claire in the figure of Eve Frame, a faded star of the *silent* screen who writes a damning exposé of her former husband.

"Go read your book in the bughouse while I swim."

The bughouse is a Bucky Fuller–inspired, geodesic-screened dome in which Philip loves to read and talk on the phone. I settle in there now for some more of James, browsing around the underlined passages of my old Penguin: "Once more, as a man conscious of having known many women, he could assist, as he would have called it, at the recurrent, the predestined phenomenon, the thing always as certain as sunrise or the coming round of Saints' days, the doing by the woman of the thing that gave her away."

Wait—what? I read on.

"She did it, ever, inevitably, infallibly—she couldn't possibly not do it. It was her nature, it was her life, and the man could always expect it without lifting a finger . . . She was the twentieth woman, she was possessed by her doom."

"Do you think twenty was a lot for back then?" I ask at dinner.

"No. I think men of the Prince's kind went to whores and lost count early in the game."

"Have you lost count?"

"Yes. You?"

"Lost it back in the rollicking seventies."

"That lost Atlantis."

"That lost Atlantis."

Nowadays I can't think of *The Golden Bowl* without seeing, superinduced on the mind's eye, rhododendron, apple trees, spruces, three giant maples half as old as the Republic, bee-laden viburnum, dragonflies skimming the pool, new-mown fields, ancient stone walls, the late slant of light. I'm told that the contents of the house are going under the hammer. A virtual auction, sure to draw a big on-line crowd. A friend has asked if I'd care to participate. Absolutely not. I wish all of those belongings, especially our golden bowl, safe passage to new homes. But a last look as they get dispersed would shatter *me* on the hearth.

In the East Room

CHAPTER SIX

THE DESTRUCTIVE ELEMENT

In 1971 the esteemed critic Irving Howe published in *Commentary*, then a journal of liberal opinion, a withering dismissal of Philip's career to date. "The cruelest thing anyone can do with *Portnoy's Complaint* is to read it twice," Howe wrote. It was "a vulgar book," no worthier of serious attention than Harry Golden's *For Two Cents Plain* (evidently a very cruel assessment). The "exceedingly joyless" author of *Letting Go* and *When She Was Good* had metamorphosed into the tawdry shock artist of *Portnoy*. Even *Goodbye, Columbus*, which Howe had previously praised, came in for revisionary lambasting.

Philip always shrugged off "the pleasure-hating Irving Howe," as he called him. Nonetheless, the glee of his revenge on Howe in the person of Professor Milton Appel in *The Anatomy Lesson* suggests how deep the by-then decade-old wound had gone. The response to Howe was more thoroughgoing than just revenge. In addition to getting even, I think Philip got the message. As he so often did with foils, he gave to Appel arguments stronger than Nathan Zuckerman's, allowed his alter ego to be bested. Tentatively, privately, perhaps confusedly, Philip's beginnings as a great American writer took shape following Howe's piece—not with the further attempts at farce that followed immediately (*Our Gang*, *The Great American Novel* and *The Breast*) but with sixty or seventy pages of manuscript from the same period that seemed to go nowhere and got put in a drawer. These had to do with a girl who blows up a building to protest the Vietnam War. From the early seventies to the mid-nineties, each time he completed a book he'd go to the drawer and reread those pages, trying to figure out what to do with them and always failing.

It was only in the aftermath of *Sabbath's Theater* that the proper inspiration struck. "I decided to create a man as clean as Mickey was filthy," he explained to me, "and decided that the girl with the bomb would be his daughter. Swede Levov, this American paragon, this stellar citizen and fulfillment of all immigrant hopes. And his daughter—a screamer, a stutterer, a *fresser* and terroristic savior of the world's oppressed." (The germ for Merry Levov was convicted Weather Underground killer Kathy Boudin, with whose parents, Leonard and Jean Boudin, Philip had been friendly.) As Philip sums it up: "This was his daughter and she was unknowable."

"On Arcady Hill Road," he tells me, "in Old Rimrock, New Jersey, the American pastoral gets interrupted by the American berserk. The strong arm of the unforeseeable, the unexpectable, the last thing you'd think, comes crashing down on Swede

Levov's fair head. That was my idea for a book. It contains, as I'd hoped, the essentials of an age— 1963 to 1974, from the death of Kennedy to the resignation of Nixon, my essential era, the time of my young manhood—and sees it all through the lens, as I say, of a man as conventionally virtuous as Mickey was conventionally wicked. What happens is that his virtue does nothing to save him. In fact, the virtuous man turns out to be far more assailable than the wicked one, far less versed in what life can do, in *how* assailable we are."

"Bellow hated *I Married a Communist*, your next book after *American Pastoral*, and wrote you a letter saying why."

"He thought no Communist lunkhead was worthy of that much attention. I tried to reason with him in my reply, tried to explain that there are two Ringolds, Ira and Murray, and between them the Cold War quarrel between Communism and liberalism gets played out."

"Maybe he'd have liked it better if you'd called the book *Ringolds*. Like *Buddenbrooks*."

"Nothing would have helped. He thought the book stank. We made up without even a falling-out. I was sure of what I'd written and am nearly as fond of that book as I was of Saul Bellow. I think I captured in it the mindlessness of American Communism: the fundamental loyalty to Moscow, the conspiratorial lying, the substitution of ideological abstraction for real life, the vast ignorance of how everyday American citizens thought and felt. And captured on the other side the baseness and chicanery of the red-baiters. Like all Communists, Ira has loved other things—his ruthless utopianism— better than truth. Likewise all the book's anti-Communist zealots, Eve Frame and the others, love their vamped-up alarmism better than truth. Both extremes believe they've cornered the market on righteousness, a better thing by far than complex, adulterated, messy, unidealized, unredeeming, unstained truth. If the book emits a warning, it's 'Beware of self-approval.'"

Meaning: Beware of purity, beware of what Hawthorne called "the persecuting spirit," the puritanical principle that put up the stocks and burned the witches. Beware of sanctimony. It survives and flourishes in matters of sex, religion, politics and race. It is the specter perpetually haunting us as a people: pseudo-redemptive dreams of ourselves washed clean of complexity, cleared of the human muck and mire. "We leave a stain, we leave a trail, we leave our imprint. Impurity, cruelty, abuse, error, excrement, semen—there's no other way to be here . . . The fantasy of purity is appalling."

Philip's denunciation of sanctimony, the "piety binge," is his answer to American sectarianism, prudery, jingoism, know-nothingism. After the Civil War, it was fantasies of redeeming an antebellum way of life and protecting the supposed purity of the white race that lit the crosses and drove the lynch mobs. Not surprising then that many of our most enduring books square up to race hatred and the self-deceptions of a vaunted, strutting white purity. Think of *Huck Finn* and *Pudd'nhead Wilson.* Think of *The Sound and the Fury, Light in August, Go Down, Moses, Absalom, Absalom!* Think of *Their Eyes Were Watching God* or *Native Son* or *Invisible Man* or *Go Tell It on the Mountain* or *Beloved.*

To this company add what seems to me Philip's masterpiece, *The Human Stain,* in which a white-seeming black man crosses the color line and lives as a Jewish intellectual, a classics professor at a New England college, till forced into early retirement when charged with having used a racist epithet in the classroom. What has happened is that he's been calling the roll for weeks. Two students have been consistently absent. In exasperation, Professor Coleman Silk says to the class, "Does anyone know these people? Do they exist or are they spooks?" The truant students turn out to be black, and the persecuting spirit promptly hounds Coleman from his job.

It was exactly the circumstance that forced Philip's friend Melvin Tumin, a distinguished sociologist of race relations at Princeton, into early retirement. Philip's exasperation at this case of political correctness run amok was the germ of the novel. But what he imagined was a black man who is not black, a Jew who is not Jewish, someone who's slipped all the punches to become himself alone. Self-invention, the supreme American act: "He is repowered and free to be whatever he wants, free to pursue the hugest aim, the confidence right in his bones to be his particular I. Free on a scale unimaginable to his father. As free as his father had been unfree."

I mentioned to Philip about the time I heard James Baldwin speak. It was at Washington University in Saint Louis, where I was teaching. Baldwin seemed prematurely elderly. He was jaundiced through the eyes. He hadn't long to live. The talk was entirely improvised though without his old improvisational skills. What was memorable was what happened in the Q and A. Someone got up and said he'd like, with the best will in the world, to speak for the white point of view. Baldwin cut him off: "There is no such thing as a white American. I defy anyone in this room to call himself white." The consternation was general, but some of us got the point. The soul of the nation is miscegenated. Blacks have taken character from whites and whites from blacks. We've been here together for a long time. "No unbaking this cake," as Philip liked to say.

"Give me Sinatra singing 'The House I Live In'—'All races and religions, that's America to me!' Give me Norman Corwin's 'On a Note of Triumph'—'Take a bow, GI! Take a bow, little guy! Each of you has a hunk of rainbow round your helmet!' There's never been a country like this one. Our idealism, as embodied in the founding documents, *constitutes* us. And belying our pride are the brutal racial facts. The disparity between who we are on paper and who we really are is what has

dumbfounded American writers and produced, between Emerson and ourselves, a literature second to
none. Hawthorne, Whitman, Melville, James, Dreiser, Sherwood Anderson, Faulkner, Bellow, they're
heartbroken patriots. Looking back now, I see it's
what I've been too."

At Philip's behest I am reading Hawthorne's al-
legorical tale "The May-Pole of Merry Mount." The
premise is that in arcadian, pre-Puritan Merry
Mount (later Quincy, Massachusetts) all was delightful, "for it was high treason to be sad at Merry
Mount." There one lived for pleasure alone. The
presiding god was Comus, child of Dionysus and
deity of revels and bawdy mirth. Merry Mounters
had come to the New World "to act out their latest
day-dream," which centered on the maypole, em-
blem of their bliss.

Into this empyrean steps Endicott, "the immiti-
gable zealot," along with his Plymouth Puritans. A
contest ensues for the soul of the village and, by
extension, all of New England—and, by further

extension, all of the New World. With little effort, the pleasure principle, in the form of the town's maypole, is felled, and a pleasure-hating regularity set up in its place. Where the pole stood, a whipping post is to be erected. Merry Mount is eclipsed by Plymouth.

"I'll take my stand forever with the Merry Mounters and their maypole," Philip says. "But of course it's the Endicotts, the purifiers, the grand inquisitors, who persist. They go to ground, they adopt new shibboleths, they reemerge. Puritanism never dies. It is immortal, our American malediction, left and right. We know it in its successive guises. We're surrounded by sanctimonious Endicotts of every stripe. Hawthorne, that visionary pessimist, already had it right: Our enemies are forever the legions of purifiers and pleasure-haters."

He told me: "I was born in the month FDR took office and knew no other president till I was twelve and the war was nearly over. The thought of him losing an election would never have entered our heads. He was our protector. That this guarantee might turn out to be provisional and reversible, that was my idea for *The Plot Against America*. I wanted to imagine my childhood exactly as it was—Herman, Bess, Sandy, me—but take away the Rooseveltian certitudes so as to steep us in the dark times of a Lindbergh, 'America First' presidency. I plunged all the familiar details into a counter-historical nightmare. I spent four years on the book, 2000 to 2004, and every night before drifting off I'd say to myself, 'Don't invent. Remember.'"

Indeed, he described the Weequahic section more completely in that book than any other. "Tinged with the bright after-storm light," says nine-year-old Philip, "Summit Avenue was as agleam with life as a pet, my own silky, pulsating pet, washed clean by sheets of falling water and now stretched its full length to bask in the bliss. Nothing would ever get me to leave here."

Reading *The Plot Against America* now, several historical contexts on from when it was written, what strikes me most is its Constitutional bedrock. At the geometric center of the book a defeated Roosevelt reemerges from isolation at Hyde Park to say to the nation: "If there is a plot being hatched by anti-democratic forces here at home harboring a Quisling blueprint for a fascist America, or by foreign nations greedy for power and supremacy—a plot to suppress the great upsurge of human liberty of which the American Bill of Rights is the fundamental document . . . let those who would dare in secret to conspire against our freedom understand that Americans will not, under any threat or in the face of any danger, surrender the guarantees of liberty framed for us by our forefathers in the Constitution of the United States."

Published in 2004, the book is a chilling prevision

of things to come. The Lindberghian proto-fascism it dramatizes, so bland and self-approving, is a demand for purity in the American ranks. "America First," in the thirties as again now, means White Christian America First. Thus late Roth added political clairvoyance to his panoply of gifts.

I swim a few laps, then dog-paddle, then just float on my back. He comes out to the pool. "Found it!" he announces. "Opened the book and skimmed for ten minutes and there it was. Goes like this and you're ideally situated to hear it: 'A man that is born falls into a dream like a man who falls into the sea. If he tries to climb out into the air as inexperienced people endeavor to do, he drowns. The way is to the destructive element submit yourself, and with the exertions of your hands and feet in the water make the deep, deep sea keep you up . . . In the destructive element immerse.' This has been my credo, the life-blood of my books. I knew it was from *Lord Jim* but didn't know where. All I had to do was put myself in a trance and I found it: 'In the destructive element immerse.' It's what I've said to myself in art and, woe is me, in life too. Submit to the deeps. Let them buoy you up."

Conrad was much on Philip's mind when he turned from long novels to short ones after *The Plot Against America*. He'd asked Bellow how to write little gems like *The Bellarosa Connection*. Bellow only laughed, as if in possession of a secret too good to share. For a more substantive answer, Philip turned to *The Shadow Line*, *Heart of Darkness*, *The Secret Sharer*, *The Nigger of the "Narcissus"*, *Youth* and *Typhoon*. "I felt I'd gone as far as I could with amplification. It was time to turn to compression, to brevity, instead. To go back to where I'd begun, but knowing things the bright young comedian of *Goodbye, Columbus* couldn't know."

The result was *Everyman*, first of Philip's four Nemeses, as he called them, in which an unnamed hero indeed stands for all of us with the same universal debt to pay to nature, the same terror of oblivion, the same cry of "Not me! Not yet!" As the fifteenth-century author of *The Summoning of Everyman* puts it: "O Death, thou comest when I had thee least in mind." "Between Chaucer and Shakespeare can you think of a better line of English literature?" Philip asks.

I tell him what's best for me in *Everyman*—his *Everyman*—is when the hero's good, loyal wife, Phoebe, catches him cheating.

"The man who's lost desire for his wife has been quite a theme for me. In *Everyman*, in *The Professor of Desire*. Zuckerman's been married—four times, is it? I assume sexual boredom and the consequent infidelities are what have moved him along in life. New to *Everyman* is seeing it all from the point of view of the wronged and outraged woman. That I had not previously tried. Phoebe's incandescent with rage, magnificent. He tells her, when caught, that he'd spent one last night with Merete, his Danish *tchotcke,* in order to break off with her. She cried all night, Everyman tells his wife, and for the rest of their Parisian holiday. 'For four whole nights?' Phoebe asks. 'That's a lot of crying for a twenty-four-year-old Dane. I don't think even Hamlet cried that much.' Oh, she's wonderful. Poor Everyman never should have betrayed her. 'I can't bear the sight of you with that satyr-on-his-good-behavior look on your face! You'll get no absolution from me—never!' That's *telling* him, Phoebe."

March 2, 2011. I have an idiopathic cough and we are in the East Room of the White House. Philip has asked me and two other friends to accompany him. He's to receive the National Humanities Medal along with numerous other talents including Sonny Rollins, Joyce Carol Oates, Donald Hall and, in absentia, Harper Lee. The honorees take their seats at the podium. Then, like thunder, the Obamas are among us. We rise. The First Lady is startling in an emerald-green sleeveless dress. I am concentrating on not coughing. Once a fit starts it can be hard to stop.

After the ceremony, we guests have full run of the first floor and I am a kid again, rushing from the Green Room to the Blue and from the Blue to the Red. I doubt I'll be back and want to get a fix on everything. The Obamas have vanished as suddenly as they appeared, but in the State Dining Room is a sumptuous buffet. I ask one of the guards to show me the elevator FDR rode in. All smiles, he obliges.

I noticed during the ceremony that when the President put the medal around Philip's neck he said something and laughed and Philip responded.

"May I ask what you two said to each other?"

"He said, 'Not slowing down, are you?' and I said, 'Oh, yes I am, Mr. President.'"

In the quiet car of the Acela that evening I

am coughing so violently that the conductor reprimands me. "You're not supposed to be sick," Philip says. "I forbid you to be sick." Next day I find out I have whooping cough. It gives him the chance to play doctor. He's immediately reading up and giving advice that contradicts my internist's. Neither has much to offer really. You grin and cough and bear it for two to three months. (Reader, get your pertussis vaccine.)

I love planetariums: the Oschin at Griffith Park in Los Angeles, the Morrison in San Francisco, the Burke Baker in Houston, the Adler in Chicago. Best is the Hayden at New York's Museum of Natural History, steps away from Philip's apartment. I tend to take in the show there before meeting him for delivered Chinese dinner on Sunday evenings. Nothing more soothing than the serenely lit blue dome and aura of cosmic piety. The audience is self-selecting. There are no bad eggs. All goes dark and suddenly the trillions of stars rain down on us. A dulcet voice says that thirteen or fourteen billion years ago all this began and that the whole shebang has another fourteen or fifteen billion years to run. Within this continuum, in an unremarkable galaxy, one of hundreds of billions, we are a vanishingly brief episode—though surely not alone in our intelligence. The universe is too big for the conditions favoring braininess not to obtain elsewhere, millions and billions of light-years away. It can't just be ice and fire up there. Still, what are the chances of hearing from our kind across eons to the nth before time is up?

"It's dark matter and dark energy that hold the show together." I'm a little overexcited by the program I've just seen. It's blunted my appetite for General Tso's chicken, which I'm pushing around. Philip offers me some of his lobster in black bean sauce.

"Eat up, Ben. This stuff on Sunday is traditional. Makes good Jews of us."

I report that the mass-energy of the universe is made up of 5 percent ordinary matter and energy, 27 percent dark matter and 68 percent dark energy. So dark matter makes up 85 percent of the total mass of the universe. Dark energy and dark matter together make up 95 percent of the total mass-energy content. The piddling 5 percent remainder is all we are capable of exploring. So far. I remind him of an epigrammatic sentence from *The Human Stain*: "There really is no bottom to what is not known."

"You're talking a lot tonight. Eat your supper." What he was not interested in, he was not interested in.

The Plot Against America was the first work he showed me in manuscript. I read successive drafts of each of the five books to come, commenting and asking questions. In the case of *Nemesis*, five years later, I provided him with my recollections of summer camp on the shores of Lake Mendota in Wisconsin. In this way my camp, Indianola, became Camp Indian Hill in the book; in this way Wisconsin became the Poconos. Not long after *Nemesis* was published, Philip received a letter noting similarities between Indian Hill and Indianola: color wars, campfire songs and the rest. Philip says in the novel that the camp owner, a widower, has bought Indian Hill in order to spend more time with his two sons. The author of the letter identified himself as Michael Woldenberg, elder son of our camp's owner, Hack Woldenberg, and asked how Philip could know so much. But while I remembered Mike and all our solemn rites, I didn't know that "Chief" Woldenberg, as we called him, was a widower. He had "Miss Chief," whom we all loved. She was, in fact, the boys' stepmother.

So the question remains: How did Philip know something that important about Indianola—that Chief was a widower who'd bought the camp to spend more time with his sons—which I could not have told him? I go on marveling at Mike Woldenberg's letter. It's proof that realistic imagination, submitting to the deeps, has an uncanny way of getting things right.

With Bellow in Brattleboro, Vermont

CHAPTER SEVEN

WHY MUST THE ATHEISTS' BOOTH LOOK SO SAD?

April 24, 2018: "Brace yourself, Ben," Philip calls to say. "Our beloved Meatball has been downgraded by the Health Department from A to B. This will ruin them! People see that sickly green B in the window and stay away." I report having seen something still more shocking at the Pan-Asian hellhole two blocks up. "I know, I know!" says Philip. "They're sporting a ptomainish, orange-colored C. A rat in a tuxedo greets you at the door."

He's on to the next thing and hangs up without goodbye. It is gratifying to hear him so exuberant. But five days later he phones to say he is "poorly"— one of his old-fashioned turns of phrase. I say I'll stay with him that night at his apartment. Around two in the morning I hear him cry out from his room. He's in trouble. I dial 911. Paramedics arrive with exemplary speed but have trouble defibrillating Philip. I can tell by the way they are talking that he could die. After an infinitely long minute or two his heartbeat reverts. We transport him first to Lenox Hill Hospital, then later that day to New York-Presbyterian, which he will never leave.

My routine for the next twenty-two mornings is to walk from my apartment to Columbus Circle and take the A train uptown to New York-Presbyterian. "What news on the Rialto?" he tends to say when I come through the door of his room. Anything can become an adventure, even a ride on the A train. One morning, a strapping young panhandler enters the sparsely populated car I'm in and says: "Ladies and gents! Ladies and gents! I am attempting to raise some *funds*, if any of you prima donnas care to help."

I report this and Philip throws back his head.
"Oh, Saul would have loved that! He'd have used it!"

"Frankly, I didn't see any prima donnas on that
train."

"Unless he meant you, Ben." It was to be our last
laugh together.

Ligt in drerd," he used to say of anyone dead.
"Lies in the ground." He admired this blunt bit of
Yiddish. "Pity our erstwhile mother tongue, spoken
by Ashkenazim going back to the time of Chaucer
and now reduced in America to stock phrases. A
European language that produced a great literature,
now consigned to Borscht Belt gags."

Like him, I can't help imagining loved ones lying
in the earth, as Yiddish would have it—the slow
processes going on down there, down where there's
nothing but what's called in *Sabbath* "the inescapable

rectitude, not to mention the boredom, of death," where you're deprived of "the fun of existing that even a flea must feel."

Saul Bellow was certain he would see his parents again after death. Philip Roth was as certain he would not. This is one way of assessing the difference between them. Who does not grasp the fierce impulse to believe? Consideration of all the ages before you existed provokes no shudder. Consideration of all the ages when you will no longer exist is simply unacceptable. How can this immense datum I am be extinguished? How can Mama and Papa be altogether gone—simply gone? How can it be that we won't be together again? How can that be? When Prince Andrei dies in *War and Peace* Natasha turns to Princess Maria and says, speaking for all of us: "Where has he gone? Where is he now?" Philip's solution was to rename mortality immortality and declare himself indestructible till death. It's not a bad gloss on what's always been the ultimate human problem.

Strolling past the Time Warner Center at

Columbus Circle one spring day a few years back, we take note of the New York City Atheists, who've set up shop under a drooping tent with isinglass windows. Within are the washed-out unbelievers purveying their pamphlets and hoping to engage you in philosophical conversation.

"Why must the atheists' booth look so sad?" Philip asks.

"Saint Patrick's it ain't."

"The big money is behind the fairy tales. All those centuries of fairy tales."

"Wish away the fairy tales and you wish away all the art, music and poetry they've engendered."

Whenever we're walking and Philip has a thought, he'll stop in his tracks. "Religions are the refuge of the weak-minded. I'd dispense with all the art, music and even poetry they've engendered if we could finally be free of them."

"The B-minor Mass? The Sistine ceiling? George Herbert's poems?"

A dog walker comes past with eight or ten

doggies of all sizes and shapes. "You see that?" he says. "Perfect concord among the breeds. The border collies admire the Heinz fifty-sevens. The Newfoundlands would make love to the dachshunds if they could. And why? Because dogs are wise enough to have no *religion*."

"We had a certain amount of God talk at our house. 'God knows whether you're lying' and that sort of thing. Was there no talk about him in your family?"

"None, fortunately. Our Zion was the United States. Our divinity was Franklin Roosevelt. My mother lit Friday-night candles, true, but only out of piety for her own mother."

"I think the Romantics got it right," I say. "They announced that God and the Imagination are one. If I had to declare a religion when passing through customs, that formula would be it."

In another mood, Philip exempted "the great reality-reflecting religion" of the ancient Greeks from his censure. He writes in *The Human Stain*:

"Not the Hebrew God, infinitely alone, infinitely obscure, monomaniacally the only god there is, was, and always will be, with nothing better to do than worry about Jews. And not the perfectly de-sexualized Christian man-god and his uncontaminated mother and all the guilt and shame that an exquisite unearthliness inspires. Instead the Greek Zeus, entangled in adventure, vividly expressive, capricious, sensual, exuberantly wedded to his own rich existence, anything but alone and anything but hidden. Instead the *divine* stain."

If the Greek gods still existed, imagine the concessions they'd set up at Columbus Circle. Atheism would have to fold its tent and slink away.

In *I Married a Communist*, Murray Ringold offers a taxonomy of American Jews. Reading it you cannot help spotting your relations: "there are the affable Jews—the inappropriate-laughing Jews, the

I-love-everyone-deeply Jews, the I-was-never-so-moved Jews, the Momma-and-Poppa-were-saints Jews, the I-do-it-all-for-my-gifted-children Jews, the I'm-sitting-here-listening-to-Itzhak-Perlman-and-I'm-crying Jews," and so on. With lightning speed they'd shed the ways of the shtetl and made themselves pillars of Americanism. They knew the brightness of their prospects here corresponded to the worst event in thirty centuries of Jewish history, that they were flourishing even as their European counterparts vanished into the abyss.

"What this country has given the Jews—" I say one evening and Philip cuts me off.

"It's what the Jews have given this country. In the sciences, the arts, in medicine, in philanthropy. And do you know why? Because night after night, year after year, decade after decade, we've gone to bed sober. It's as simple as that. How could we have avoided the resentment of our hard-drinking Gentile brethren? Did I ever tell you about my dealings with that dipso Capote?"

He had indeed and has performed the playlet for me. In act one, he is at home watching Johnny Carson when Truman comes on and explains that culture in America is under the thumb of "a Jewish mafia that runs from Columbia University to Columbia Pictures." In act two, Philip, seeing Capote at George Plimpton's a few weeks later, corners him and says: "I saw you on *The Tonight Show* and take the gravest exception to what you said."

"Nothing I can do about that!" says Truman and flits away.

Curtain.

"What a *dope* I was to let him get off a line like that and vanish into his golden cloud. And me left to my umbrage. No, the author of *In Cold Blood* had no use for earnest, striving, Jewishy Philip Roth. My name was not in the New York Social Register and I didn't know how to drink or even smoke a cigarette."

Plimpton had been among Philip's first Gentile friends. "I thought they'd all be like that," he says with a laugh. "His sleekness and lightly held entitlement and *insouciance* were a revelation. His books of 'participatory journalism' pioneered something—a self-deflating style of autobiography born of supreme self-assurance."

After reading in manuscript *Exit Ghost*, the final novel narrated by Nathan Zuckerman, with its eight-page excursus on George, I showed Philip an extraordinary photo I'd found. In it Plimpton is seated at Elaine's, the now-defunct Manhattan restaurant famed for superior clientele and ghastly food. Revelers surround George. It looks as though the fun will never stop. Everything Zuckerman had fled from when he retreated to the Berkshires is summed up in the glamour of that image. "Here is the cover of your book," I said. "This photo is full of the enticements that Nathan, that ghost of a man, gave up for art." But the photographer foolishly drove a hard bargain and Philip decided against the image. I still wish he'd shelled out the extortionate fee. That would have been some book jacket.

Zuckerman, who narrates nine of Philip's books, is overwhelmingly an embodiment of iron discipline and self-denying artistic aspiration. The young acolyte we meet in *The Ghost Writer* metamorphoses into the scandalously successful author in *Zuckerman Unbound* and *The Anatomy Lesson* and *The Prague Orgy*. When we meet him next, in *The Counterlife*, he's married for a fourth time, to Maria Freshfield, and expecting a child. Wives one, two and three Zuckerman had dispatched with an airy phrase in *The Anatomy Lesson*: "the puzzle of passionless marriages to three exemplary women." In *The Facts*, published after *The Counterlife*, Maria is still expecting. Seems like quite a long pregnancy. What it really seems is that Philip had no particular interest in Nathan's amatory or conjugal life—to say nothing of his parental prospects. (Easier to imagine Garbo with a baby than Nathan Zuckerman.) He stands for artistic struggle, not love or marriage or parenthood, and the realist who made him quite casually dropped the ball when called upon to give his hero-narrator a convincing marital history.

In *Exit Ghost*, our hero, having earlier told us of Swede Levov, Ira Ringold and Coleman Silk, now returns, Rip Van Winkle–like, from his long years alone to a vastly changed New York. The year is 2004. Zuckerman is so cut off as to have barely heard of 9/11. Everything puzzles him. Having consecrated himself completely, year in and year out, to the turning of raw life into words on the page, he is a revenant among flesh-and-blood people— but a revenant longing for one last outburst of feeling, one last bit of unwritten, untransformed, "real" life. Nothing doing. Experience is over for him, long since. He's been impotent and incontinent for years, a man removed, as Philip puts it in an interview, "from all turbulence, from all his deeds and misdeeds and the distraction of the pursuit of happiness—the depicter, rather, of other lives, whose personal trials and historic travails come to possess his imagination entirely and feed on the strength of his mental energy."

After several days he flees New York as rashly as he arrived. Thus Philip says goodbye to Nathan Zuckerman, his intricate invention. "Gone for good" are the final words of the book.

Passing by Columbus Circle on May 20, 2018, the day it became apparent that Philip would not recover—a lovely spring day, a gift of a day, a day lacking nothing—I looked in vain for our atheists. Gone for good? Their place had been taken by the Lyndon LaRouchians with pictures of their current hero, Donald Trump. (Three years earlier they were displaying images of Obama with a Hitler mustache.) I am a man slow to anger who, once there, may turn violent. Anyhow, here is what happened next: I ripped down one of the pictures.

"Mister, *please!*" cried a LaRouchian. I pushed their "literature," you should pardon the expression, off the table and into the gutter, where it belonged. "Call the cops!" another LaRouchian implored passersby. They just laughed. But I was not laughing. I was in a fucking rage. And grieving. And spotless as the lamb.

The studio in summer

CHAPTER EIGHT

PARTINGS

We were little children in the Depression. We saw fear in our parents' eyes. It made workhorses of us." Philip is talking about himself and John Updike, his friendly rival for half a century. "Still writing on his deathbed. Poems. A book review. None of this retirement stuff for John."

This retirement stuff had its shadow side. In one mood, Philip would declare that the demon of art had turned loose of him and he'd never been happier. On other occasions he'd say, "A great dynamism has left me and I feel it." The days were very long. He missed the bonfire he'd been.

He kept in his safe in New York all that was required for suicide should he find himself too disabled to go on: pills, a plastic bag and band with which to affix it to the neck. Also a box of Triscuits. He'd been told of people throwing up after taking the barbiturates on an empty stomach. "I want you to know that a day may come when I'll need your assistance, if only to hand me those things from the safe. You'll be in no legal jeopardy. I've checked on that."

I only hoped I wouldn't be called into play. "That box of Triscuits will need changing from time to time." I say the silliest things when nervous.

"Let's not worry about the Triscuits. Just pay attention to what I'm telling you."

End of sex. End of writing. He saw the end of life rearing up, was determined to meet it clear-eyed. A tenet with him was to take deliberate leave if disabled. The moment at Presbyterian when he decided, on May 21, to ask that life support be removed came—I saw it on his face—when a hospital sub-intern, sugarcoating nothing, told him he'd never swim again. Philip wanted no more of life on such terms. He wanted to make a rational exit.

I asked if he'd prefer to die back at West Seventy-Ninth Street. "No," he said and did not say more. But I think he feared going home to his chair, his books, his bed. The lure of life might have reasserted itself.

In the summer of 2017, Philip's last summer, he'd proposed that we read a book together, *My Confession*, in which Tolstoy writes: "The thought of suicide came as naturally to me then as the thought of improving life had come to me before." Every night before bed, Lev Nikolaevich would remove from his room the length of rope with which he might hang himself from the crossbeam.

"I thought of hanging myself in the barn," Philip told me. "I got to be afraid of going in there. You've been in the dark too. Have you read a better description of it than Tolstoy's? When I knew I'd become a danger to myself in the spring of 1993, I went to New Canaan and checked into Silver Hill. The breakdown was complete. I was in physical and mental agony. It was the lowest point of my life. With *The Counterlife*, *Patrimony* and *Operation Shylock* to my credit, I could find no grounds for going on. This was also when my marriage to Claire ended. She visited me there and I told her I wanted a divorce."

"Silver Hill saved you?"

"A girl I met there saved me."

Philip was open with people about his orthopedic torments, guarded about his cardiac illness, deeply secretive about his mental breakdowns— unless, as with the Halcion-induced madness he'd suffered in 1986, he could blame a drug company. "Upjohn's little miracle pill," he called the later-banned drug. Gingerly, I asked about his thirty-six days at Silver Hill.

"I fell in love with a delightful person. Juvenile-looking but with a battered soulfulness that was not at all childlike. And with a little bell-like voice that drew me. We've been together one way and another ever since. In different circumstances we'd·have married. I expect she'll be in the room when I go."

"Well, that's a long way off. Let's not talk about—"

"I'd like to know you'll be there too."

Philip was a great proposer of marriage, to this and many another delightful person. (Just not to the two women he actually wed. They proposed, browbeatingly, to him.) He would propose in jest. He would propose in earnest. He would propose in town and in the country. He would propose on brief acquaintance. He would propose on condition that there be no patter of little feet. In his seventies he would consult with doctors on the odds of fathering a defective child, and then propose.

Best was when he proposed to Věra Saudková, Kafka's niece. She'd lost her position in a Prague publishing firm in 1968 after the Russians rolled in.

When he called on her, she let him sit at Kafka's desk and browse the family albums. "I know a way to get you out of Czechoslovakia," he told her. "Will you marry me?" She graciously declined, saying Prague ("the little mother with claws," Uncle Franz had called it) was her only possible home.

"Turned me down flat. Who the hell was she waiting for?"

To say Philip stopped writing is inaccurate. He stopped making art. But his old way of coping with any embattlement, to sit down to the keyboard, continued in the years of his retirement. The underside of his greatness swarmed with grievances time had not assuaged. He couldn't stop litigating the past and produced over a thousand pages of—well, what to call it?—self-justification in those years, all of which I read.

He'd been giving me typescripts and manu-

scripts since we met, a habit that accelerated. Sometimes these would be birthday gifts, sometimes
gifts for no occasion. Sometimes he'd make jokes
about the market value of such items when he in-
scribed them: "For your old age!" Sometimes he'd
rather solemnly address me as if I were his
archivist.

On one occasion he handed me a full-scale book
called "Notes for My Biographer," which would
shortly be announced for publication before being
withdrawn. The text is a point-by-point effort, fre-
quently self-deceiving, to refute all of Claire
Bloom's charges against him in *Leaving a Doll's
House*, whose publication Philip counted among the
worst catastrophes of his life and credited with his
failure to win the Nobel. She'd assailed him and he
needed to defend his moral reputation, pocked and
homely though it was.

Another typescript, entitled in some copies
"Notes on a Scandal Monger," sought to even the
score with his earliest anointed biographer and

afterward ex-friend, Ross Miller, dedicatee of *The Human Stain*, who he felt had betrayed him by failing to work effectively and in a timely way on the project. People who should have been interviewed died off while Ross dithered. This is the sad tale of someone handed a job for which he was ill-equipped. And then featured as a villain. Ross was no villain, only a literary amateur, and it pained me to hear Philip go on about him as if he were Iago. "You cast him in a role much too large," I said more than once. "He wasn't malevolent, only not up to the task." But as with Maggie and Claire and Francine, so with Ross: The appetite for vengeance was insatiable. Philip could not get enough of getting even.

He gave me both these bulky typescripts, the fruits of his retirement. After withdrawing "Notes for My Biographer," he asked me to destroy my copy. I returned it to him instead. "Notes on a Scandal Monger" (it does not bear this title in my version) I kept with the mass of other documents in my Roth file.

What to do with such things when an author dies? There are essentially three possibilities: You can throw them away. You can leave them to the misunderstanding or neglect of heirs. Or you can get them to an institution that knows how to care for such things. I deeded my entire collection to the Manuscripts Division of Princeton's Firestone Library. Parting with it put a calm in me. I knew the papers would be secure for as long as Princeton stood, as safe there as if they were Whitman's or Melville's.

Notable in Claire Bloom's bill of particulars was her allegation that Philip's ailments were sometimes imaginary. But I was one of his medical proxies and can testify that they were all terrifyingly real and that his stoicism in the face of them was beyond what I, whose rude health he admired and teased me about, could have summoned. Still, there were limits. He liked to quote an unemphatic line from Hemingway's "The Snows of Kilimanjaro": "He could stand pain as well as any man, until it went on too long, and wore him out."

It was in basic training at Fort Dix that a first and lasting injury befell him. "Another grunt and I were on KP and carrying a large kettle of potatoes. He dropped his end, causing me to wrench my back. I saw stars and felt a searing pain. It was this injury that led to my honorable discharge after one year."

"You know, when my father died I wanted an honor guard at his funeral. They asked first to see the discharge. I looked in drawer after drawer and file after file and finally I found it in his billfold. He'd been carrying it on his person since the autumn of '45."

"I understand that perfectly. Whatever else lay

ahead, I felt my honorable discharge was a plaudit that could never be taken from me—however lamed I was, arriving at the University of Chicago the following year in agony and with a back brace under my Brooks Brothers suit."

It was the start of a history that would lead from surgery to surgery, including three spinal fusions in the last fifteen years of his life. He said the third, which restored an inch or two of the height he'd been losing, made him feel he was carrying inside himself a replica of the Eiffel Tower.

I'd been instructed beforehand to test his recall after each of the anesthesias. More than anything he feared cognitive loss. "Philip, who was FDR's Secretary of Labor?" I asked him in recovery.

"Frances Perkins."

"And of the Interior?"

"Harold Ickes."

"Remember his middle initial?"

"L."

"You're all there."

He then proceeded to his usual test of himself, the prologue to *The Canterbury Tales*: "Whan that Aprille with his shoures soote / The droghte of Marche hath perced to the roote," and so on for some lines more.

Prescribed painkillers in ever larger doses produced expectable results. The fentanyl patch he wore was crazy-making. In combination with other culprits it drove him over the edge. One night in the country, at about three o'clock in the morning, he entered the guest bedroom and said, in tears, "Ben, can you find out for me if I'm awake or asleep? Can we call somebody to find out?" I walked him back to his room and stayed till sunup.

Withdrawal from fentanyl and other narcotic analgesics would be the great unspoken trial of Philip's old age, an additional illness.

Add to it the epic struggle with heart disease. When told in 1982 that he had a fraction of normal cardiac function, he began the ritual of putting all his work in clear order at the end of each working

day, not knowing if he'd return. "I was more afraid
for the work in progress than for myself," he told
me. He kept the knowledge of this Damoclean
sword almost entirely to himself. The humiliation
of impotence, a side effect of the beta-blocker he
was given, was not the least of his anguish. He
begged for bypass surgery but was repeatedly told
he was not a candidate.

Then in August of 1989, at fifty-six, after swimming only the first of his afternoon laps, he felt
overwhelmed and in immediate peril and wondered
if he might actually precede his dying father to the
grave. Twenty-four hours later, a quintuple bypass
was performed at New York Hospital. Philip felt
newborn. "I would smile to myself in the hospital
bed at night," he writes in *Patrimony*, "envisioning
my heart as a tiny infant suckling itself on this
blood coursing unobstructed now through the
newly attached arteries borrowed from my leg.
This, I thought, is what the thrill must be like nurs-
ing one's own infant—the strident, dreamlike

postoperative heartbeat was not mine but *its*." There in the ICU he'd won the goal of happiness complete. He was free of the time bomb that had been ticking in his chest.

This new leasehold was also the proximate cause of a creative rebirth, probably the greatest in American literary history. What followed the experimentation of *The Counterlife* and *Deception* (a minor, radio play–like novel completed shortly before his bypass) was a sequence of masterpieces: *Patrimony, Operation Shylock, Sabbath's Theater, American Pastoral, I Married a Communist, The Human Stain, The Dying Animal, The Plot Against America, Everyman, Indignation, Exit Ghost* and more, including his masterly last bow, *Nemesis*.

Further cardiac procedures followed. In 1998, he was back at New York Hospital for renal artery angioplasty and insertion of a stent. The following year, his left carotid artery was opened. A year after that came another angioplasty and stent insertion. In 2003, he was transferred in terrible pain from

Charlotte Hungerford Hospital in Torrington to Lenox Hill Hospital in Manhattan, an event he loved describing: the rickety old ambulance, the bumpkin drivers. They'd never been to New York and Philip had to shout directions the whole way. They unloaded him, still in a hospital gown and on his gurney, at Lexington and Seventieth. "Is this neighborhood safe?" they asked. Curious passersby stopped to stare. Only the usual autograph hound was lacking. This indignity went on for fifteen long minutes before the drivers figured out that Lenox Hill was one block over and six up.

Next day, a defibrillator was installed, a raised rectangle about the size of a pack of cigarettes under the skin of his chest. "What do I need this thing for?" he used to say, skeptical of its merits. "I need this thing like a bus needs a parachute." Then one evening he fibrillated and the thing went off, knocking him for a loop and restoring his heartbeat. He got the picture of what it was for, even grew fond of it. When the mechanism wore out and had to be replaced he said he was going to sell the old one on eBay. "Could get a *pret*-ty penny for it."

Philip required more and more angioplasties and stents. Then, in 2013, it became clear that his ramus and LAD arteries were completely occluded. He was once again a walking bomb. Three or four interventions reopened both. Further interventions were required to reopen them yet again.

His doctors never felt these were losing battles. Cardiologists are optimistic, can-do people and Philip's were among the best. In September of 2016 his aortic valve was replaced with either a bovine- or porcine-based substitute. I could never get that part straight. I asked in some trepidation about the body rejecting such tissue and was told the chances were zero. For some reason though, the idea of a piece of pig or cow in his heart kept me up nights.

I should have been worried about other things. The recuperation did not go smoothly. By early November he was back in New York-Presbyterian to treat blood clots that had formed on the leaflets of the new valve. On the evening of November 8, I breezed in with the word on the street: It would be an early night with Hillary taking Florida and Pennsylvania and Michigan.

He gave me a torpid look and said, "I'm scared."

First my vehement youth, all fight and craving," he told me. "Then this so suddenly—old age telling me to have a long last look. I've come through. I'm on the other side of all battles. Aspiration, that beast, has died in me. Whenever death comes to mind I tell myself, 'It is now and here we are,' and this suffices. So long as we're alive we're immortal, no?"

Immortal for now, while I last, is this humblest of memories—Philip waking me on a summer's day with a shave-and-a-haircut knock and favorite song of his: "You can always tell a *Yank*, by the way they call him *Hank*, by the way he *talks* and the way he *thinks* and the way he likes to buy you *drinks!* You can always tell a *Yank!*" He was full of joy on the good mornings. When I got down to breakfast, there he'd be, presiding and singing: "You can always tell a *Yank*, by the way he hates a *crank*, by the way he *shows* that he's not *afraid* to get up and call a spade a *spade!* You can always tell a *Yank!*"

Memory is where the living may rejoin the dead. There they anoint us. Through memory we obtain the blessing. Through memory we remain filial. Memory makes us Jacob, not Esau. "You can always tell a *Yank*, by the way he drives a *tank*, to defend a thing called *democracy* and put an end to *tyranny!* You can *al*-ways tell—a *Yank!*" This book has been a partial portrait, of course. There is really no bottom to what is not remembered. I have only such fragments as I've shored. But Philip is abundantly present as I write this. I can laugh and commiserate with him. He's invisible to me now but omnipresent, like the stars at noon. At our leave-taking I said, "You have been the joy of my life." "And you of mine," he replied. I bent forward. He briefly put a hand on my head.

Some months later I dream I've forgotten how to tie my tie. Over and under? Under and around? Under and over and back again? None of these work. Then he looms up behind me in the mirror, reaches over my shoulders, knots a perfect half-Windsor. I wake to no pall on the day. For I am here and it is now, and what I would not part with I have kept.

IMAGE CREDITS

The Hue and Cry at Our House
A Year Remembered

After John F. Kennedy's speech in front of the Hotel Texas in Fort Worth on November 22, 1963, he was greeted by an eleven-year-old Benjamin Taylor and his mother waiting to shake his hand. Only a few hours later, Taylor was told of the president's assassination. Recalling the tumult as he saw everything he had once considered stable begin to grow more complex, Taylor reflects upon the impact our larger American story had on his own.

"This acute, intense memoir achieves the stature of national as well as personal elegy, a breathtaking achievement, classical and impassioned."
–Patricia Hampl

 PENGUIN BOOKS

Naples Declared

A Walk Around the Bay

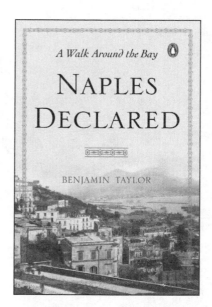

Gracefully written and full of good humor, *Naples Declared* presents a compulsively readable account of three thousand years of Naples history. From the Catacombs of San Gennaro to the luminous paintings of Caravaggio to the ruins of Pompeii, renowned author Benjamin Taylor takes readers on a stroll around the city Italians lovingly call Il Cratere.

"There is no more witty, worldly, cultivated, or amiably candid observer imaginable than Benjamin Taylor. This book belongs on the shelf of the very best literary travel guides." –Phillip Lopate